CHARLES A. ARCHER

~

EVERYBODY
PADDLES

~

A LEADER'S BLUEPRINT

FOR CREATING A UNIFIED TEAM

GREENLEAF
BOOK GROUP PRESS

Original publication by BookBaby, New York

Copyright © 2014 Charles A. Archer
This edition published by Greenleaf Book Group Press
Austin, Texas
www.greenleafbookgroup.com

For ordering information or special discounts for bulk purchases, please contact
Greenleaf Book Group at PO Box 91869, Austin, TX 78709, 512.891.6100.

Design and composition by Greenleaf Book Group
Cover design by Greenleaf Book Group

Cataloging-in-Publication data
Archer, Charles A.
   Everybody paddles : a leader's blueprint for creating a unified team / Charles
A. Archer.—Third edition.
   pages ; cm
   Originally published: New York : BookBaby, c2012.
   Issued also as an ebook.
   Includes bibliographical references.
   ISBN: 978-1-62634-101-2
   1. Teams in the workplace. 2. Organizational behavior. 3. Personnel manage-
ment. 4. Consensus (Social sciences) I. Title.

HD66 .A73 2014
658.4/022   2014940771

Part of the Tree Neutral® program, which offsets the number of
trees consumed in the production and printing of this book by
taking proactive steps, such as planting trees in direct proportion to
the number of trees used: www.treeneutral.com

TreeNeutral

Printed in the United States of America on acid-free paper
14 15 16 17 18 19 10 9 8 7 6 5 4 3 2 1
Third Edition

TO THE EDCSPIN STAFF

CONTENTS

~

CONTENTS

Foreword

THE BOAT

~

Peter F. Borish

Every once in a while, though usually infrequently, you meet someone, slap your forehead, and say, "I sure wish I had known this person well prior to today." For me, Charles Archer is one of those people.

Given my background and passion for both early-stage start-up businesses and innovative philanthropy, I invariably have too many people requesting a meeting to ask me for something. You can imagine how refreshing it was, early into our initial lunch, for Charles to be the one offering *me* inspirational conversation, insight, and passion on a host of issues. Within a few minutes I, too, had jumped aboard the "Everybody Paddles" boat.

One of the central tenets of *Everybody Paddles* is that in an environment where each of us can be isolated yet technologically connected, a successful and balanced life requires non-digital interaction with others. An essential ingredient that just about every author who contributed to this book mentions is the inclusion of a mentor. The ingredient that is often missing from digital mentoring is emotional connectedness. This intangible is too easily turned off if the sole connection is through a power button. Needing to be responsive, responsible, and resolute with a mentor assists us in getting over the hump during the inevitable stretches of frustration or rejection.

I view engagement in philanthropy as a perfect example of the need to be physically rather than simply technologically engaged. Imagine if all you did was read grant proposals, rank them, and then allocate scarce dollars—without a site visit—to meet those in need. You could wait for the numbers to come back to try to determine if, indeed, you have made an impact. Yet wouldn't it be so much more rewarding to roll up your sleeves, take the time, and make the effort to visit the programs you intend to assist? In other words, do due diligence and be a mentor!

Of course, when you become an active participant, there is the chance of failure. Charles suggests, and I agree, that we cannot run away from failure. We must embrace and learn from it. But in isolated digital space, it is too easy to run away from failure. As I said, hitting the power switch is too easy. Virtually every successful entrepreneur has experienced what I call a "park bench day." Disappointment is to be expected when we're rejected after an interview, when we're told a business plan is not good enough for funding, or when we're passed over for promotion. After a particularly tough day, it is acceptable to go sit on a park bench and ask, "How or why am I in this situation?" But it is acceptable only for the remainder of the day! Those who learn from rejection get up off the bench and get back into the game. Others give up and feel emotionally cleansed, since the cause of their stress has been removed. However, they haven't left open the possibility of future success. The Everybody Paddles concept is a journey, not a destination. The park bench is often a resting stop along the path.

After resting, we paddle and paddle, with the assistance and support of others. The Everybody Paddles movement is an exponential function; its rate of growth accelerates as more people assist others in removing obstacles to success. Charles Archer is on to something here. I am honored to have been invited to climb aboard.

PREFACE

When I became director of a large Brooklyn-based social service agency in 2007, I knew little about management. I was a lawyer and a lobbyist. In those roles, other people made the leadership decisions. I participated and watched, but I didn't have the final say-so. Suddenly I was in charge, and hundreds of employees looked to me to make the important decisions.

I quickly began to learn management techniques on the job. I also discovered that most managers go through the same process. Getting an MBA is nice, but it does not really prepare anyone for the realities of day-to-day, real-life actions.

As a result, I decided to find books that provided realistic guidelines for someone like me or, for that matter, any executive charged with providing leadership. But I found very little. All of the management books offered advice, but not enough seemed connected to what really happens inside an organization or an office.

That's why this book came to be written. *Everybody Paddles* examines all aspects of management, from creating the original vision to communicating it to your team, with practical guidelines based on real experiences. What I learned grew into guiding principles that have helped my agency grow and maintain its position as a model for other social service agencies throughout New York. These principles will also work for any executive in any industry.

I'm a firm believer in sharing knowledge. Management is all about identifying important issues and making the best decisions. I hope this book is useful to CEOs and other managers who are striving to be better.

Introduction

BUILDING CONSENSUS WITH THE "EVERYBODY PADDLES" CONCEPT

This is a book about team building and leadership. I had spent some time working on how to express these concepts in a clear, concise way when the solution came to me one day as I glanced at a magazine. I was attending a conference at the time, and at that point in the schedule we were supposed to be networking for the benefit not only of ourselves but also of our organizations. Somehow, the networking party just got out of hand. Things happen. So, I walked into a vacant room, sat down on a couch, and flipped through my phone messages. That's when I saw it: a photograph of a whitewater raft on the cover of a sporting magazine.

There were five people in the raft as the river raged on, threatening to capsize them all. They were all leaning into their oars at the same moment, however, and were executing, as if in one complete, unified movement, a turn to avoid the face of a huge rock in front of them. The water parted in a V formation, splitting into two white jet streams, and all eyes were focused on the right-hand side. The intensity of their focus got to me, as well as the sense that they were all executing that one turn in total cooperation. No one was sloughing off—unlike the conventioneers at the raucous party outside. A life-or-death turn, executed perfectly, in unison, by five people.

"Everybody Paddles" became my slogan from then on. (There's a saying in my office: "Charles is crazy. Don't get in his way when he is passionate about something!") This idea had captivated me.

A few days later I was back at the Evelyn Douglin Center for Serving People in Need (EDCSPIN), the Brooklyn non-profit organization I cofounded in 1996, where we handle about $25 million a year in services for the disabled community, and I imagined paddles everywhere—all over the walls—as a symbol of this newfound image of unity. I found a store that sold me a bunch of paddles, and the next day I started nailing them to the walls. To this day they cover the premises. A few days after that, I took a magic marker and walked around our space—a large floor in an old customs building near the Brooklyn waterfront—and started writing on the paddles: "Everyone Paddles in the Same Direction, at the Same Time, Toward the Same Goal."

I see this as a process that goes far beyond my social service agency. There's no reason it can't include individual families as well as communities, cities, states, and countries. That's because Everybody Paddles represents a pattern of growth, development, and improvement that occurs when all participants work together for a common interest.

This concept is very important today. As we all know, society is divided by economics, education, classism, ageism, gender differences, religion, and partisan politics. Despite these challenges, I believe there is opportunity for unity because everyone shares the desired outcome of benefiting from a common interest.

It does take everyone working together to achieve a common goal. Yet I also recognize that we are individuals. As a result, the Everybody Paddles concept would seem to contradict the American mantra of self-dependence and individualism. It doesn't. Let me explain why.

Great thinkers have often stressed individuality. I love a famous quotation from Hillel—one of the greatest sages in Jewish history—that encapsulates so much of what I want to say in this book:

"If I am not for myself, who will be? If I am only for myself, what am I? If not now, when?"[1]

With this perfect wording, uttered in first-century Jerusalem, Hillel was saying what I had been thinking all the while as the CEO of a social service agency: Stand up for yourself. Take responsibility and act as if you are alone during the crucial fights and moments. But also always remember that human beings need one another, and "the other person is you." When individuals with integrity join together with others of equal stature, they can paddle forward in confidence, trusting one another, to achieve what they set out to accomplish.

Hillel introduced the concept of individuality, getting people to think about who they were. But according to historian Jacob Burchardt, it wasn't until the Late Middle Ages—toward the beginning of the Renaissance, the time of rebirth of Western culture—that the concept truly began to catch on.

> During the Middle Ages the veil covering human souls was a cloth of faith, biases, ignorance and illusions . . . in so far as the human being was considered only as belonging to a race, a population, a party, a corporation, a family or any other forms of "community." For the first time, it was Italy that [broke] this veil and dictated the "objective" study of the State and other worldly things. This new way of considering reality aside, it further developed the "subjective" aspect, and man becomes "individual," spiritual, assuming his new status' consciousness.[2]

America was founded soon after the end of the Renaissance in Europe by bold individuals who dared to sail thousands of miles across dangerous seas to an unknown land. As a result, Americans have always prided themselves on rugged individuality and acclaimed anyone with that perceived personality: mountain men and heroic soldiers Daniel Boone, Kit Carson, and Sergeant Alvin York come to mind.

The concept is stressed in our times. Donald Trump, a somewhat controversial businessman and developer who has helped many people lead productive lives, said about leadership, "You are a one-man army."[3] I agree. Yes, you are when you need to be.

The promotion of individuality, however, is only a façade. The web that unites us becomes clearly visible during tragedies, such as the terrorist attacks on September 11, 2001, or the Boston Marathon bombings on April 15, 2013. In both cases, communities around the country banded together to show their solidarity with the victims in each great city.

The same thing happened during the Iranian hostage crisis in the late 1970s, when yellow ribbons served as the symbol of American unity. Our individual opinions and political differences were smoothed over by the desire to present a united front as Americans.

Americans may talk about "I" but are acutely aware that the better pronoun is "We." We often work as individuals in a group setting. That approach provides opportunities for creativity while helping the organization reach toward its goal.

To promote this reality, I outline strategies that have been proven to modify attitudes, capabilities, and efforts, acknowledging that everybody within a given company must actively participate in the advancement of that company's mission, vision, value structure, and deliverables.

To add practical experience to each principled approach, I have asked thought leaders and influencers to contribute their accounts of building consensus. These unique perspectives on the principles outlined in the book appear at the end of each chapter.

By the time you have finished reading this book, you will have a blueprint for building and maintaining company consensus. You will know how to make sure that everyone on your team is inside the boat, paddling with singular focus toward the desired destination.

Principle One

UNITY STABILIZES THE BOAT

~

Focusing on individuals who are building teams inside an organization raises two important questions: (1) What separates us? and (2) What brings us together? (The goal of the second question is so we can work hard and achieve great things.)

Every organization—whether a group, a company, an association, or any other entity that relies on the cooperation between its members—is simply a collection of individuals. As a result, the success of any organization depends totally on individuals. Obviously, most of us want to achieve success both on an individual and on a group level. We identify with success: Winning sports teams gain followers, for example. WE win, not just the team.

An excellent organization has quality people who have been allowed over the course of their lives to develop great qualities like independence (responsibility), creativity (permissive flexibility), and accountability (getting the job done), but who can also cooperate and subordinate themselves when necessary to the mission at hand inside the organization. So, the core requirement of team building is a certain amount of freedom that both develops an individual and creates collective discipline. Unfortunately, not every organization can do that. And this brings us back to the first of our two fundamental questions.

What Separates Us?

There's no question that we have a hard time working together, whether in our families or on the job. According to the most recent U.S. Census Bureau report, the divorce rate of first-time marriages is 41 percent; second marriages, 60 percent; and third marriages, 73 percent. That's a lot of dissension.

Some of that comes from our upbringing. For most of us, the pronouns we were most familiar with were *I* and *me*. Conversations typically emphasized how much *I* wanted to accomplish my career goals, how stressful the whole process was for *me*, how I could better a better *me*, and so on. Country singer Roy Clark encapsulated this notion of total self-absorption in his popular 1969 song "Yesterday, When I Was Young."[1]

Early in my career, the more I focused on where I wanted to go, the less I focused on ways to achieve the success I craved.

As I matured, however, I began to realize that *we* meant much more than *I*.

Another element that often keeps us apart involves how we perceive one another. Humans developed as members of small clans, and anyone not within that family unit was considered an enemy. We now have developed far more sophisticated relationships, but our brains still contain the primitive elements inherited from our hunter-gatherer forebears.

Us vs. We or They

As a result of how we perceive one another, we inherently assign everyone to a category, either We or They. "They" are everyone else who looks or acts a little differently. So, for centuries, groups of people have been discriminated against by other groups because of their gender, ethnicity, religion, age, or socioeconomic class. This blind prejudice has led to inequality, mass murder, and enslavement.

Our country is no exception. Throughout U.S. history, we have witnessed great periods when every American has been asked to align him- or herself with American values. These usually occurred during times of war or injustice: For example, during World War I and World War II, women were asked to support men particularly by working in various industries; during the civil rights movement, to secure equality for African Americans, women rallied for constant unity at home, at work, and in the voting booth; and, most recently, after 9/11,

Americans united against world terrorists. That's why President George W. Bush's ringing declaration that you are "for us or against us" struck such a chord with so many people. That same attitude spiced up the Vietnam War era, when bumper stickers proudly proclaimed "America: Love It or Leave It."

In the United States, the divisions have often focused on gender, sexual identity, and race. Discrimination has often resulted. Individuals are defined as *they* are stereotyped and isolated from the rest of the society, which believes *they* are nothing more than the embodiment of the perceived notions of those who consider themselves a superior *we*. Within our society, discrimination is rampant and on most occasions crippling, effectively demoralizing people without reason.

I know about this firsthand. I was an individual inside a family, and I was also part of a larger group of the local community. We lived inside the dangerous Brooklyn projects, but it was clear to outsiders that as a family we were different. We stood out by certain peculiarities in our behavior.

What probably set us apart most from American blacks inside the projects was our West Indian blood. My mother is a black woman from the southern United States; my father is a black man from Barbados. We walked in and out of the buildings in single file, like a small military regiment, played together, and kept to ourselves. My parents and grandparents were strict, and I learned to be the same with my brothers and sisters: I was usually telling them what to do. We participated in our own Caribbean culture-based church groups that were very tight communities. As a result, the neighbors usually left us alone.

My separation continued as a black man in the legal profession and as a CEO among my middle managers and coworkers. I learned that how I handle the perceived differences is critical to my own well-being and success.

I also found that there is a fine line between being different and alienating the larger group around me. Every social organization around me tends to be tribal in some way, and I stand out in any number of ways, including by being different culturally or professionally or because of my social status or religious affiliation. And there are subtribes within the tribes. The way I talk or dress is often enough to stir animosity or suspicion if I inadvertently cross the line into another group.

Those distinctions begin to fade, however, once we realize that we really aren't different: We are all trying to survive every day. After all, today through genetic research we know there's no such thing as race. In fact, there's no *we* or *they*; there is only *us*. We are all the same, divided only by our own individual abilities and not by any artificial aspect of appearance, religion, or gender. We are not forced to limit ourselves or anyone else with these manufactured perimeters.

As the Indian philosopher B. R. Ambedkar said, "We have liberty in order to reform our social system, which is full of inequality, discrimination and other things which conflict with our fundamental rights."[2]

The Generation Gap

A third element that separates us involves generations, each of which is different. Back in Ancient Greece, Plato complained about the younger generation of his day. In truth, though, at that time there wasn't much difference between one set of children and the next. Most of humanity lived similar lives for centuries: Sons followed fathers into professions; women learned to be housewives. But that's not really true anymore, at least on a behavioral level.

That consistency was shattered in the nineteenth century as factories began siphoning children off from farms and creating the urban sprawl of modern society. The differences became even more apparent in the twentieth century. Famed newsman Tom Brokaw wrote about Americans who endured the Depression followed by World War II, calling them the "Greatest Generation" in his popular book of the same name. People who lived through such cataclysmic turning points didn't complain; they survived.

The next generations, however, were catered to and pampered. The excesses of the 1960s, tempered by the Vietnam War, reflected the results of overindulgence. The process has continued, creating what New York City behavioral scientist Deborah Bright names "entitleists." They shun responsibility for their own behavior. Of course, they happily take credit for any good things that happen. They rarely see how their actions affect others. They don't see themselves as part of a team, but rather as individuals with others around them. They expect promotions and raises based totally on their presence, not their actions.

Their children are even further from what had been the norm. Generation Y, also known as the "Millennials," consists of 80 million young people born between 1980 and 1995. They represent the fastest-growing segment of the American workforce today. In many ways, Gen Y varies greatly from any previous generation. For starters, they were born in a world awash in technology. They don't know anything else and consider their parents woefully ignorant in that area. For them, cell phones, computers, and the Internet are necessities and have always existed. They are always connected via headphones or earplugs, their eyes riveted on some screen.

Divided by Technology?

In a recent AT&T commercial, the camera revealed people everywhere listening to music playing through their phones. They were in crowded libraries, on the subway, at the beach, or walking down the street, completely oblivious to their surroundings. In October 2009, for example, there was a subway shooting in an American city. A madman chose a victim at random on a train. No one noticed the gun, though the shooter went so far as to wipe his nose with it several times as he taunted people verbally. No one looked up from their smartphones or iPads.

At work or at home, day or night, Generation Yers check their Facebook pages and read email on their iPhone, Black-Berry, or other device. There is no difference between work and private lives; they get personal email, instant messages, texts, and tweets in both places. Their parents isolated the public and private parts of their lives, but Gen Y doesn't see any distinctions.

Millennials also expect immediate answers and instant gratification. They know every piece of equipment and eagerly snap up the latest innovation to come onstream. As a result of that need for immediacy, most recent college graduates are unhappy employees. For example, University of New Hampshire management professor Paul Harvey found that members of Gen Y have a "very inflated sense of self" that leads to "unrealistic expectations" and, ultimately, "chronic disappointment."[3] Their only interests, according to a separate report in the September 2010 *Journal of Management,* are "high salaries" and "lots of leisure time off the job."[4]

I remember interviewing one young person for an entry-level position. He couldn't write; he simply didn't know how to put two words together in any form. I asked him why he didn't learn even the basics during his years in high school and college. His answer was that he expected his secretary would do his writing for him.

"What happens if you don't have a secretary?" I asked. He wasn't sure (but I knew for certain he wasn't going to have a secretary at our agency).

He didn't get the position he applied for, nor was he unusual. Members of Gen Y have been brought up with everyone telling them that they are great and that they can conquer the world. They believe it. They expect to be the boss the second day after joining some organization. They figure they'll magically float to the top of the ladder. Naturally, with such lofty, implausible goals, they are easily prone to disappointment.

The problem may be simple: Maybe they are just misplaced. Many people have taken jobs they just aren't suited for simply because they needed to find work. That doesn't mean they can't be motivated or capable in a job they like and can handle.

A manager's responsibility is to put an employee in a place where he can achieve the best results. That's the mantra of coaches in sports as well. Successful coaches use the strengths of their team to build success. A baseball manager who relies on home runs to win would be hard pressed to rack up victories with a team long on speed and short on power.

I take that same approach with my agency. Some people

might not be good social workers; they may not enjoy working with clients or have the patience necessary to aid disabled clients with severe needs. However, they may be superb in arranging for treatment and identifying resources. They can be vital members of a team by contributing where they can help the most and achieve the most satisfaction at the same time.

Employees who like what they are doing are far more content. "If you're engaged, you know what's expected of you at work, you feel connected to people you work with, and you want to be there," wrote Dr. Jim Harter, Gallup's chief scientist of workplace management and well-being. "You feel a part of something significant, so you're more likely to want to be part of a solution, to be part of a bigger tribe. All that has positive performance consequences for teams and organizations."[5]

However, any employer has to recognize that today's employees are not the same as those of previous generations and to be willing to understand the differences. Gen Y members are fully capable of doing anything; they just work differently. They need to set short- and long-term goals. Helping them do that is part of my job. They also have to realize that goals change; they evolve, just as mine did. I set out to be an accountant and shifted to law, only to end up running a social service agency, which, it turns out, requires knowledge of both accounting and law.

Technology advances are also separating us into haves and have-nots. As I mentioned, Gen Y members in general have no problem with technology; they know—and often purchase—all the most recent upgrades. Many others, however—from both the younger and the older generations—are not as comfortable with high-tech devices. They either can't afford the latest innovation or simply lack interest in learning how to use it. These persons are increasingly relegated to lower-paying, less glamorous positions while silently envying the successful characters portrayed on television and in the movies.

No doubt, there are factors in addition to those outlined above that keep us subdivided. It's all too easy to figure out what keeps us apart; the second fundamental question is harder to answer.

What Brings Us Together?

What brings people together so that we can work hard and achieve great things?

Leadership

One clear answer to this critical question is leadership. Unfortunately, there is a lack of skilled leaders in workplaces today. A recent Gallup poll found that 70 percent of 100 million full-time workers in this country hate their jobs and often are "roaming the halls, spreading discontent." Earlier surveys from 2008 and 2010 show that negative attitude virtually has not changed despite the passage of years.

Why? Gallup pinned the blame for the majority of

disengaged and uninspired workers on bosses who are simply not doing their jobs well. "The managers from hell are creating active disengagement, costing the United States an estimated $450 billion to $550 billion annually," wrote Jim Clifton, the CEO and chairman of Gallup.[6]

Cheryl Connor added in a *Forbes* column: "These employees need better leaders who know how to inspire and motivate them, give them opportunities for development, and treat them with the respect and dignity they each deserve. A third of a person's life is spent in the workplace, sometimes more. If the environment an employee works in is led by an extraordinary leader who cares about their development, it leaves employees with little room to complain."[7]

Leadership involves more than just giving often-irrational orders, the favorite ploy of the blowhard boss in the comic *Dilbert*. Instead, leadership involves such areas as communication and identifying others who also have leadership abilities.

I learned that lesson after I became a lobbyist for an organization that represents social service agencies. I had been with the Brooklyn district attorney's office for three years when friends and colleagues recommended I take a job as a lobbyist. A longtime lieutenant of the director, a woman named Louise, was retiring after twenty years. When Louise's choice for the job declined the offer, I was next in line.

I quickly learned why no one else would take the position. For starters, the apartment I occupied when I was in Albany to talk to legislators couldn't have been a more depressing place. It was in a decent location, but not well maintained.

Next, when I tried to discuss the matter with Louise (she had taken a similar position at another company, which meant that we were in meetings together and working on similar issues in Albany), I discovered that she was a bully. She came from privilege—with parents who were wealthy, hardworking, yet elitist types—and she felt entitled. Sadly, her idealism was her justification. While putting herself forward as the central voice for those with disabilities, she simultaneously disabled anyone around her who attracted her disapproval.

Like me, she was a lawyer and a zealous advocate for non-profits serving the disabled community. It must be said that she did get results as a lobbyist for nonprofit organizations, which are not allowed to lobby legislators directly for funds. Out of the office, after work, she was kind and pleasant. But at work she was more inclined to set up a guillotine than to discuss anything. She eliminated teamwork in order to build herself up as a singular hero, a stifling approach that prevented those around her from growing.

I worked on pins and needles all the time. She chipped away at my self-esteem. I was battle hardened from my years in the DA's office, but Louise was too much for me; I was afraid of her.

The three years I worked under her were intense, but I learned a lot—some of it from her negative example—about being a leader and about myself. I realize in retrospect that I could have done several things differently: (1) by showing more confidence in myself; (2) by asking more questions and demanding more support; (3) by taking more initiative; (4) by continuing my education; (5) by writing better reports and becoming a better inside player; and (6) by confronting Louise when I needed to.

Becoming a Better Leader

I try not to make those mistakes in my job now, and I understand my employees better because of my time under such a leader-dictator. In addition, I came up with one important realization: First and foremost, leaders need followers. How can anyone lead in isolation?

Jesus had an impact only because of his followers, who carried his message to the rest of the world. Louise tried to run the organization alone but ended up simply forcing people to leave or curtailing their abilities to succeed. In the end, the organization suffered right along with her opportunities for greater success.

The way a leader approaches her job and the people she leads determines the success of an organization, but it can also predict failure. At the end of the day, the success of an organization is based on the collective achievements of every member, not just the leader. The functions and responsibilities of every person, as well as every person's ability to achieve the goals set forth by the leader, are essential to the organization's success.

This can be accomplished only through effective communication. In order to articulate the mission, purpose, values, and objectives of an organization, a leader needs to be a skilled communicator. Effective communication is the means by which leaders can achieve their objectives, whether in a business, a family, or elsewhere. The leader must constantly be in "messaging mode."

There should never be a moment when the leader has not taken the opportunity to share important information. From meeting with staff to networking in the community to using social media and pursuing speaking engagements, a leader must constantly communicate his goals and expectations while demonstrating collaboration.

Of course, not everything should be public knowledge. Information should be shared on a need-to-know basis, but if those who need to know don't, then the entire structure is threatened by inefficiency and potential mistakes.

As a CEO, I also realize that every organizational system involves cooperative activities. Among these are the following:

⋄ development of staff or a staff member by
  supervisors and managers;
⋄ a course of action staff must adhere to and duties
  they must complete; and

◇ an exchange between employees and their supervisors, and between the CEO and the management team.

A process is involved in every aspect of a business. And each of these cooperative activities must be developed, monitored, and maintained through a process; that is, the manner by which the utilities or departments meet the organization's central goal. An organization cannot run efficiently if a proper and comprehensive process is not in place.

Every process in an organization must include these five factors:

1. an objective
2. a function
3. integrity
4. transparency
5. compliance

As leaders, our approach is always to develop policies, procedures, and processes that will bring the desired result. However, this cannot be the only approach. We must consider what we will do when the policies, procedures, and processes are not followed.

For example, some processes might state that signatures are required on purchase orders and requisition forms. Guess what? A form was submitted without the appropriate signature. A new process must be put in place through which both the person who places the order and the finance clerk thoroughly review each submission.

No system is foolproof. Nonetheless, the leader must consider potential lapses in the operating system.

Mistakes happen. However, they can be considered teaching opportunities rather than an opening to execute someone. We all err, but the goal should be to determine where the process failed and then provide a solution.

Finally, every member of a staff must have specific and measurable responsibilities. Success is attained through the leader's conduct. It is the leader's responsibility to (1) make expectations clear; (2) monitor progress or the lack thereof; and (3) effectively respond to obstacles and shortcomings. This will ensure optimal success in an organization's functioning. Responsibility involves choices, motives, attitudes, foresight, education, training, and professionalism. Conversely, responsibility is about accepting the task of leading the collective unit, in whatever form or context. The responsibility has to be that I/we will do what is right and appropriate; I/we will conduct myself/ourselves within ethical and legal standards; and I/we will acknowledge if our behavior does not support those beliefs.

The core values of a leader are based on his or her integrity; namely, that part of an individual that no one knows in detail but that everyone hopes is good, positive, and moral. It's the part of the individual that must be progressive and demonstrate restraint in given situations, moments, and challenges. This core depends on trust. When signs of shortcomings are observed, disbelief becomes the reality. Top leaders attain enduring success and prominence through professional will and personal humility, accepting criticism as an advantage en route to realizing achievement. Leadership is not about control, being correct, or telling others what to do. Leadership is about nurturing those who are willing to follow you as they, themselves, become better leaders.

Developing New Leaders

Leadership involves developing subordinates who are capable of assuming some of the leader's duties as well as securing a successor. It has been said that if you aren't training your successor, you aren't providing effective leadership.

The first step in this process is identifying a potential leader. This person should not be ego driven. She is instead receptive to feedback, expecting comments rather than turning away or simply denying responsibility. Flexibility is also important, since everything changes; a leader must be able to shift too. A good leader wants the best results, no matter who gets the credit. Being able to share guarantees a better cultural fit. Every organization has its own culture. A leader accepts that culture and is willing to adapt to it and, if possible, improve the negative aspects.

One of the three cornerstones of my agency comes to mind in this discussion about cultivating leaders: my assistant executive director of programs. Along with the assistant executive director of administration and the chief financial officer, she is someone I depend on, because I travel a lot and need employees who can take on leadership roles. I delegate. I must have an executive team who can make good decisions without waiting for me to direct them. Some decisions can't wait.

My assistant executive director of programs was not anyone's idea of a leader at first. A southern black woman, she was shy and rarely spoke. I saw that she was reliable and that her clients loved her. I really thought she could become a leader, although I doubt she expected to be put in that role since, initially, she was perceived as more of a supporting actor.

She resisted the idea at first, so I moved slowly as I groomed her to become a leader. I would encourage her and give her small tasks. For example, she would take my place at a meeting I could have attended, but where I wanted her to have the responsibility of representing our agency. Over time, I gave her more responsibility. I asked for her opinion on major decisions and tried to treat her like a partner.

As the feedback loop expanded, she felt more confident that I was not just listening to her opinion for form's sake, but respecting what she had to say and acting on it. She now holds a prominent and important position. She's responsible and incredibly capable. Today she is a role model to many of the women on our staff. They treat her as the leader—and that's fine with me.

The same process can work with an entire organization or just a couple of people. As Sun Tzu, the noted Chinese general and strategist of the seventh century, wrote in *The Art of War*, "Managing few is the same as managing many." This is an intriguing thought for any leader—profound, really. Imagine a pyramid-like structure of power that just keeps moving up to a single man or woman or a small board of directors with handpicked officers who manage hundreds or even millions of people.

I have learned something else about leadership: knowing when to engage, and when to stand back and say nothing. This is a skill that I developed with seven frenetic brothers and sisters who were all screaming to have their needs met— not at every moment, but certainly at every other moment.

They helped me learn when to fight and when not to. I learned Muhammad Ali's "Rope a Dope" and other defensive techniques. I learned that a strong person is also wise and does not need to use conflict all the time. You observe patterns around you and learn when to disengage from inappropriate behavior. For example, I learned not to waste energy on insignificant situations—to pick my battles.

The new leaders are waiting for us. Many young graduates want to be in charge, make decisions, and lead companies. It's our job to guide them and help them understand that leadership comes with a price.

Noted humanitarian Helen Keller, who overcame profound disabilities, once said, "Life is either a daring adventure or nothing."[8] It takes courage and determination to take the adventure, and even more to see it through. Courageous leaders experience as many obstacles and as much fear as anyone else; they just don't let it paralyze them. They accomplish this by replacing "I can't" with "I will," and this allows them to continue.

Overcoming the Tendency Toward Separation

As freethinking people, we can modify our social systems to incorporate the fundamental and unalienable rights of everyone. We can end discrimination by working as individuals toward a common goal. After all, the efforts to suture the wounds within society—notably the civil rights movement, the feminist movement, and so on—have been led by strong individuals such as Dr. Martin Luther King Jr. and Betty Friedan.

Alongside these leaders, we can work together to dismantle the societal norms that justify discrimination. Eradicating prejudice within our society begins at the most basic levels of beliefs and ideologies. Historically, there has yet to be a society that exists without discrimination or micro-aggression, but that does not mean it cannot be done. As children, we don't automatically know about discrimination and prejudice, being fearful or biased against someone because of their skin color or facial features or culture. Those are learned behaviors, taught and modeled and passed down from older generations to younger ones. Oscar Hammerstein II made this abundantly—and cleverly—clear in his heartrending lyrics for the song "You've Got to Be Carefully Taught" from the Broadway musical *South Pacific*.[9]

Working together, we can do away with the destructive forces of prejudice and discrimination. Instead of grouping individuals into categories, we must appreciate diversity, encourage individuality, and practice unity. We can set the example for our children who, in turn, will produce generations who no longer see people of different backgrounds or life experiences as part of anything else but the human race. At that point, there will be only *us*, each holding a paddle and moving toward a common destination.

Teamwork: Some History

Teamwork has been the norm in industry since the late 1700s. That's when inventor Eli Whitney, better known for his cotton gin, came up with the idea of an assembly line to assemble guns for the U.S. government. Before that, society stressed individual creativity and effort. Sure, artists like Michelangelo had assistants, but he did most of the work and sculpting. You don't think of him—or any other prominent artist, writer, or leader, for that matter—as part of a team.

The Industrial Revolution of the 1800s, with the

introduction of steam power and then electric energy, forced everyone to turn to teams. Individuality was replaced by unions and massive factories where teamwork resulted in the production of products. Henry Ford, the auto magnate, helped refine the system by perfecting the assembly line to produce cars cheap enough for the average consumer.

Americans have been on a teamwork kick ever since. Bruce Piasecki, author of *Doing More with Teams: The New Way of Winning*, explained the need for teamwork this way:

> Teams expand the human experience. They extend our wings in practical, pragmatic, and measurable ways. People who would not normally be able to succeed alone—the planners, the doers, those who lack the internal spark to market themselves—can reap the benefits of success in the context of teams . . . Teams are more important in a global economy than they've ever been before. Standing out in a crowded marketplace takes constant innovation and the ability to get fast results. With the complexity of today's workplace, even the most brilliant individual is not likely to have the skill set to take projects from start to finish. The ability to collaborate is everything, and that requires high-functioning teams.[10]

The concept sounds great, but in reality, many people are very selfish. All of us have the tendency to be egotistical, even though many of us may not be willing to admit it. We often just get so caught up with *I* that we don't notice the *we*. The challenge then is to realize that we will go much further if we channel our energies into forward movement rather than attempting to travel the road alone.

Even individuals who seemingly achieved success based on their own efforts, such as inventor Thomas Edison, really didn't. In Edison's case, people sponsored him, encouraged him, and finally helped promote his inventions. The same thing happens with great artists.

I recognize this truth in my own life. I learned all about teamwork as a kid growing up in Brooklyn with seven brothers and sisters. Both of my parents worked away from the house all day, so we had to handle the chores. As the eldest, I got up early to make sure everyone got off to school, and I babysat at the end of the day. All of us had our assigned roles in the family.

My family is very religious. As a result, I also read about teamwork in the Bible. For example, Deborah, a prominent Israelite leader in the Book of Judges, didn't call for just one tribe to fight the Canaanites; she invited all the tribes to work as a team. In the New Testament, I read about how the disciples also worked as a team to spread the Gospel.

I also worked on teams with classmates. My high school

relied on team teaching, which we thought was the way to even up the sides between teachers and students. When I graduated, I became even more aware of the importance of teamwork. I could never have become an attorney without the assistance of family members who encouraged me, teachers who tutored me, and colleagues who helped motivate me. I just didn't notice how many people were involved in my success.

Now, as head of a major social service agency that provides assistance to mentally and physically disabled residents throughout New York City, I am acutely aware of the teamwork that's necessary to get help to the people who need it. Social workers, direct care staff, and administrators have to work in unison to achieve the optimum results.

◆ ◆ ◆

With good leadership, any group of employees can learn to work together. In the related, brief "Perspective" essay that follows, Kennedy Swaratsingh speaks about necessary unity among the Caribbean Islands. "The message of the 'Everybody Paddles' movement resonates with me," he says, "because I would like to impress upon the leaders of this region the need to focus on a common goal and then ask ourselves what we need to do to go in the same direction." Kennedy has a valid point. Whether the "team" is made up of a group of individuals sharing a common mission or a group of islands sharing common economic goals, nothing happens until everybody is in the same boat, paddling in the same direction with coordinated effort. I admire Kennedy's grasp of the challenges and importance of forging teams across national and cultural boundaries.

PERSPECTIVE: UNIFICATION OF THE CARIBBEAN REGION

Kennedy Swaratsingh

I first met Charles A. Archer in Barbados at the launch of an earlier edition of *Everybody Paddles*. I then had the opportunity to chat with him after reading the book, and I realized that the concepts in his book were very close to my own philosophy.

I spent twenty years as a Catholic priest in Trinidad, also serving as a chaplain in the Defense Force. I was also a member of the Parliament of Trinidad and Tobago.

My philosophy has always been that we are not divided by the Caribbean Sea but rather that we are united by it. Because of our size and geographic location, we should be more inclined to work as one family, moving in the same direction. My political and philosophical underpinnings are corroborated by Charles's book.

Here is a dollars-and-cents example: We replicate things in each island that we could build once and use often. Instead, we build it three, four, five, or six times. From an economic perspective, this is rather inefficient.

The formation of the European Union postdated our regional experience of unity. There was an earlier attempt to form a similar federation in the Caribbean that did not get off the ground. We do have CARICOM, a regional group where we try to work and negotiate as a region, but for a number of reasons we continue to be challenged by issues of sovereignty and isolation. So, ironically, an American traveler can come into our islands with only an ID card, but Caribbean citizens still need passports to go from island to island. These examples exhibit symptoms of disunity and dysfunctionality.

In fact, the only two real enduring examples of Caribbean unity are the West Indies cricket team and the University of the West Indies. Otherwise, we compete as individual nations for the same business, sometimes to our own detriment.

When I was younger, I participated in a youth group where we used to sing "United We Stand, Divided We Fall." In the Caribbean, we have not learned this lesson. I feel that the Caribbean will not attain its full potential until we have learned to celebrate our unique differences as something to be encouraged and embraced and not as something to divide us. And we must also learn to take collective advantage of our strengths.

For example, the landmass of Guyana has enough acreage to feed the entire Caribbean, while Trinidad has sufficient energy to help the entire region manage its energy costs, yet we cannot seem to find a way to leverage the best of what each island brings. So, as a regional consultant, I try to find ways to utilize the talent of the region. We need to develop leaders, but more importantly, we need to develop a philosophy that guides what we do. There must be a commitment in the region to moving in the same direction, coming together and coalescing around certain fundamental principles.

What holds us back from doing that? Certainly, sovereignty is a sticky issue. Particularly in difficult economic times, as elected officials revert back to what is good for their own islands, we have become more protectionist. Thus far, elected leaders of the region have lacked either the will or a way to harness the collective talent and energy of the region to move it in a particular and determined direction.

My graduate study has focused on leadership, emphasizing how Caribbean island nations can use the modern tools available to them in order to prosper. We continue to pay more for goods and services than we would if the region were more connected. For that to happen, elected leadership needs to focus on sustainable development. We cannot afford to continue to be left behind by a world that is moving forward at a much greater pace.

The message of the "Everybody Paddles" movement resonates with me because I would like to impress upon the leaders of this region the need to focus on a common goal and then ask ourselves what we need to do to go in the same direction. We have to overcome our "island mentality." The wonderful familiarity of small-island living can be accompanied by a very limiting parochial perspective. As I learned from my service as a chaplain in the Defense Force, talk gets you only so far. It wasn't until I participated in drills as a regular member of the army that I was accepted. One of the things I had to learn was to let others in the group lead me, knowing that we were all in it together, working toward a common goal.

If we could just get the countries of the Caribbean to unite in pursuit of their common interests, one can only imagine the possibilities for what I believe is the greatest region on Earth.

Principle Two

PURPOSE PROVIDES PROPULSION

~

Although EDCSPIN is a successful social service agency today, it didn't start that way. The agency began as an idea. Growing up, I had seen a lot of people who needed help. Some disabled individuals lived in my apartment building, some in the neighborhood, and some attended my school. I saw how they struggled to obtain daily necessities. Their burdens did not decrease over time, adding pressure to both the disabled persons and their families. Today, an estimated 18 percent of the population has to cope with one or more disabilities. I always wanted to help but was in no position to do so.

During a family trip in 1995, I read about social service agencies in a magazine and decided to see if I could start one. I didn't want to run it; I wanted to create an agency that could continue to provide assistance even if I were no longer actively involved. At that time, my vision was limited to a simple idea:

Find disabled people in need and help them. On the surface, that seemed sufficient—a decade ago. However, the more I became involved in the day-to-day running of the agency, the more I realized that we needed much more: We needed a mission statement and a vision statement.

Definitive Mission

It's important to understand that a mission statement and a vision statement are not the same thing. A mission statement defines the organization's purpose and primary objective and is written for employees and our core audiences. A vision statement also provides a definition of purpose, but with an emphasis on the values of an organization.

I thought these documents would be easy to write—especially the mission statement. After all, I had established my own mission statement years ago: to become a lawyer. I stuck to the goal even though I had to take other jobs en route. I was very persistent.

As I looked at the agency, I certainly could see we needed a mission statement. Employees were eating in the back room, ignoring clients, and making a mess. They punched in and out without any set schedule. No one knew where anyone was.

But knowing we needed a mission statement was no help in actually preparing one. After all, I was a lawyer who had become a manager; I didn't learn from a textbook, but inch by inch through practical experience. I was confident, inspired by Dr. Martin Luther King Jr.'s comment "Faith is taking the first step even when you don't see the whole staircase."[1] I certainly had faith in my abilities, though, and so I began by using the same skills I had learned in the district attorney's office.

I began by reading a variety of mission statements by major corporations.

Having gathered that information, I researched the various definitions of a mission statement. In particular, I liked the one given in *Entrepreneur* magazine: It "captures, in a few succinct sentences, the essence of your business's goals and the philosophies underlying them. Equally important, the mission statement signals what your business is all about to your customers, employees, suppliers and the community."[2] That made sense. But what was our "business all about" at EDCSPIN?

We still wanted to help people, of course. But that didn't give a true picture of the agency's efforts. I ended up writing a series of questions that had to be answered by the mission statement. They included:

- ◇ Why were we in business?
- ◇ Who were our customers?
- ◇ How did we want customers to see us?
- ◇ What did we actually do?
- ◇ How were we different from other agencies?
- ◇ What were our values?

With that questionnaire to work with, the executive team and I began to thrash out the wording. We ended up with a long—but compelling—mission statement that encapsulates our agency:

Evelyn Douglin Center for Serving People in Need's mission is to enhance the quality of life for persons with disabilities and their families.

We BELIEVE that all members of society, with or without disabilities, are entitled to respect and equal opportunities.

We EMPOWER our consumers to strive toward their highest potential, and prepare them to deal effectively with the challenges they may face.

We PROVIDE every service in a spirit of excellence and genuine caring.

We PLEDGE to develop programs and provide services to hard-to-serve individuals, in un-served and underserved communities.

We AIM to be a leader in providing quality, comprehensive services.

We STRIVE to build a better future for the people we serve, today!

We posted our mission statement in our office for employees to see every day and on our website. This mission statement gives our staff a guideline for how to conduct themselves in the office and with clients, a standard that we all strive to meet.

Completing the mission statement represented the first half of my plans. The second half involved the vision statement, which carries more weight than the mission statement since it goes beyond the agency's boundaries.

Vision = Action Plan

Just as with writing our agency's mission statement, I had never worked on a vision statement before, even though I had a personal one. Like most people, I had thought about my future. As I mentioned earlier, I was originally going to be an accountant. I don't know where that career plan came from; perhaps a high school teacher suggested it. Regardless, that was my vision. It changed while I was in college, however, when I realized I could do more by becoming an attorney. I began to focus my energy in that direction and eventually achieved the goal.

Life is funny that way. After getting my law degree, I pictured myself in a glamorous position in the entertainment industry or corporate law. Instead, I'm working with the disabled, learning compassion and humility along the way. Instead of visiting posh mansions, I'm spending my days in the poorer parts of our community. I could never have foreseen that. The Mexicans have a saying: "If you want to make God laugh, tell Him your plans!"

My initial efforts at the agency were concentrated on stabilizing it, rebuilding trust, and reaching out to the community. I was too busy multitasking and managing to think about the agency's vision. And even without a clear vision statement, my—our—efforts were effective. We gradually became more successful and socially important. We began to provide services to clients considered some of the hardest to help: sex offenders, criminals, and the like.

However, as our agency expanded, I realized that we needed a real vision to carry us into the future. Once more I sat down and wrote a list of questions that a vision statement would have to answer.

- What does *successful* mean?
- How do we measure that?
- How do we know when we've achieved it?
- What does *socially important* mean?

Communication, discipline, setting standards, and the like are all vital to the survival of an organization. However, as I asked these questions, I soon realized that a vision is even more significant; it is really the most important element in the success of an agency. Vision provides the framework for everything our agency does. The most successful companies in the world have clear visions that allow them to function smoothly.

Creating a vision statement may be the most important function of a leader. A vision holds everyone together, offering a kind of picture of what success looks like. It helps answer the questions that every employee asks about the company, including its goals, position in society, and value. It is coherent: a set formula that won't mutate under pressure or the passage of time.

A good vision inspires people. It helps winnow out ideas that don't fit, since the only opportunities we consider are those that help us achieve our vision, while others can be discarded. Vision provides no blueprint to the future, but it does explain the destination: Where are we going, and how will we get there?

In studying the vision statements of other companies and organizations, I realized that a vision really has two parts: an ideology and an envisioned future. The *Harvard Business Review* called them the yin and yang.

The yin in this approach represents what we stand for and why we exist. It is unchanged: the Ten Commandments of any organization. The yang is the vision of what lies ahead that keeps any organization together regardless of the changes around it. To some, it is the moral philosophy, the "way" that an agency functions.

An organization's yin, or the core values it stands for, helps it endure across decades in an ever-changing society.

The authors of the *Harvard Business Review* article "Building Your Company's Vision" noted:

> William Procter and James Gamble didn't instill in P&G's culture a focus on product excellence merely as a strategy for success but as an almost religious tenet. And that value has been passed down for more than 15 decades by P&G people. Service to the customer—even to the point of subservience—is a way of life at Nordstrom that traces its roots back to 1901, eight decades before customer service programs became stylish. For Bill Hewlett and David Packard, respect for the individual was first and foremost a deep personal value; they didn't get it from a book or hear it from a management guru. Ralph S. Larsen, CEO of Johnson & Johnson, puts it this way: "The core values embodied in our credo might be a competitive advantage, but that is not why we have them. We have them because they define for us what we stand for, and we would hold them even if they became a competitive disadvantage in certain situations."[3]

On the other hand, the yang, the envisioned future, shows what an organization wants to be, the goal the staff strive for that sometimes requires flexibility in response to outside changes in order to reach it.

As I said, there was no real vision when I arrived at the agency. Everyone worked hard, but without a sense of direction or purpose. I had to spend a lot of time in a lot of meetings with department executives and employees, but we developed a vision that sustains us now.

Breaking It Down: Steps Toward Defining the Vision

The process of creating a vision is not really complicated, but, as with developing a mission statement, it does take time to get the wording right and to focus properly. Above all, the vision must be real and felt by the leadership, not merely a concept that fulfills an image. A core vision is rooted primarily in the best people in an organization, those accountable for building it—mined from the deeply moral aspects of personality, from our deepest principles. Vision is not necessarily something imposed from the outside, from books, or through other people's ideas.

After all, we all have visions and dreams. But men and women working on a corporate vision can get sidetracked into discussions of their future retirement or plans to start a family. In our meetings we had to concentrate totally on the agency's future.

Where did we expect to be in ten years? Twenty? How were we going to get there? That was the vision we had to see and explain.

First, we had to pick a target year because what we could envision for ten years ahead might be totally different for a hundred. We decided to look five years into the future; that seemed like a nice compromise. Five years may seem like a long time, but it really isn't.

Meanwhile, through my research, I found out we were pretty typical. Organizational visions run from two to ten years, with five years being a convenient middle ground.

We started the actual creation process by looking at what we had accomplished. In the ten years the agency had existed, we had helped thousands of people. We had won several community awards and achieved some positive coverage in the media. These were things to be proud of. These awards and the other recognition become the stepping-stones to future success. They provided the positive platform that a vision could be built on.

Once we knew how long a period of time the vision should cover and some of the high points we hoped to expand on, we then wrote the first draft. Some people like to agonize over every word. In reality, the first step has to be a creative process. We simply tried to articulate as quickly as possible what we envisioned.

The process allowed for open brainstorming. No

suggestion was ignored. Some of the proposals just didn't seem right; others were perfect—we just knew it. Everyone in the meetings had his or her own personal concept of the agency. By articulating them, we were able to see how different they were.

I opened the first session by telling my team members that we were going to compose something important. As a result, we had to imagine a grand future, not something small and insignificant. That can seem scary, but a good vision has an element of fear in it; fear drives us to succeed. I think of Dr. King's "I Have a Dream" speech. That's a real and, in some ways, outlandish vision. Yet, slowly, American society is beginning to achieve it. I wanted something that lofty for our agency.

I told them that we were all busy, so we didn't have years to struggle with this. We needed to work fast, to put into words what all of us were thinking. I wanted them to develop the vision in under an hour. More than that, and we would have been bogged down in picayune word choices and petty differences.

To go fast, we had to reach deep within and draw out our hidden thoughts. It didn't matter to me what other people thought as long as they relayed their hopes and aspirations: the ones nestled deep in their hearts. I also needed them to look ahead. They could not be mired in what was happening right then, but at what could happen, what they wanted to happen. They had to pretend that, in fact, the agency had succeeded. What would be the ideal situation? That's what the vision should encapsulate. It also had to be personal: What did you want to see happen with your position? The personal element feeds into the overall agency vision.

Although computers, iPads, and other devices have created a high-tech world, I deliberately used a blackboard for the meeting. I wrote "Draft" as a title and then wrote key words down for everyone to see. My colleagues were not intimidated by the throwback method and were very open with their comments and suggestions. I grew to appreciate their understanding of the agency and how they struggled to create a coherent image of it.

Once we had our first version, we put it aside for several days and then met again to reexamine it. Several of us noticed something missing or perhaps a possible word change. I would estimate that most of the original vision survived, but some alterations were made.

Our biggest discussion centered on specificity. A vision statement can be very detailed, after all, or it can be annoyingly vague. Visions require clear definitions that allow some kind of measurement. Saying "we will see more clients," for example, is not as motivating as "we will double the number of clients helped in the next five years."

Once the vision statement had gone through a series of drafts, I circulated the final version to people in the agency and presidents of other agencies, regulators, and various opinion leaders outside the agency. They were not as involved with EDCSPIN and thus could offer an unbiased reaction. Employees typically nod their heads and pay little attention; I needed more input than that.

As with our mission statement, we ended up choosing a long—but equally compelling—vision statement. The expanded version on our website reads:

> EDCSPIN's focus is providing individuals with developmental disabilities and/or mental retardation the opportunity to learn skills needed to reach their highest level of independence, while insuring they experience the same privileges and opportunities enjoyed by all members of our society.

> In pursuing the mission of Enhancing the Quality of Life for Persons with Disabilities and Their Families, we pledge to conduct ourselves according to the following values:

PERSONS WITH DISABILITIES FIRST

We will measure everything we do against a simple standard: is this good for the persons with disabilities we serve? If not, we will not do it.

INTEGRITY

We will honor the trust of the families of those we serve and those who pay for our services. We will conduct ourselves ethically and within the law at all times. We will communicate honestly.

RESPECT

We will act with fairness at all times. We appreciate the need to balance work and family life. We respect individual differences. We welcome open communication and promote inclusiveness.

OPPORTUNITY

We value teamwork and the need to have everyone paddling at the same time, in the same direction, toward the same goal. We want our employees to grow so the reach of our good works can also grow.

We seek to recognize effort and achievement and to express gratitude for jobs done well.

ACCOUNTABILITY

We are accountable for the proper use of funds. We are committed to transparent reporting that is so essential to healthy and trusting relationships.

TOGETHERNESS

We value each other and believe no one's role is more important than another's. We are all about serving those in need and we are all in this together, working to enhance the lives of those we serve.

"Make It So": Implementing the Vision

Once we had developed the vision, we began the process of promoting it. We wanted everyone to buy in, to pick up an oar and join the rest of us who were already paddling.

At our next staff meeting, I presented the outline. To many people, a vision statement is just empty words; they have already heard such talk before. I demonstrated its importance in my approach, keeping direct eye contact and expressing myself enthusiastically. That kind of energy can be infectious.

I also had to challenge the staff to read the vision statement and to accept it. They had to know that following the vision required effort. It forced them to change, to match their actions to the vision. They also had to understand what the vision meant. I am direct and use a vocabulary that's appropriate for my employees. Buzzwords have their place, but not in a frank discussion.

In addition, I let the employees know what specific tasks, actions, and behaviors I expected them to do to be sure the vision had meaning. Our vision statement easily translates into day-to-day activities.

Most importantly, I told them how the vision statement served as my guideline. In that way, I modeled use of the vision and demonstrated that it really did have a purpose.

Nevertheless, it took a while to sink in. Staffers had spent years doing what they thought was best. No one was working together in the kind of cohesive action needed for real success. The vision served as a guideline, but only after employees began to see how it allowed them to pull together.

But once the mission and the vision statements were fully integrated into the team culture, everyone finally began to paddle in unison.

◆　◆　◆

Theodore Hanley, a doctor from Saint Kitts, writes in his "Perspective" essay about making things happen, being committed to one's work, and helping others. He says, "Medicine is an excellent vehicle for making change and helping other people make changes. I enjoy doing that more than anything else. In my own life, I've made things happen. I enjoy learning." In other words, Dr. Hanley has a firm grasp on his vision—medicine as a vehicle for positive impact—and as you will see, he has pursued that vision relentlessly, drawing others into his mission of healing.

PERSPECTIVE: LEAVE YOUR IMPRINT EVERYWHERE

Theodore Hanley, MD

I was born in 1960 in the countryside in a place called Tabernacle, in a mountainous area on the Caribbean island of Saint Kitts. I was the eldest of five children:

three boys and two girls. My mother was the district head nurse and a midwife until we moved to Saint Peters. My parents decided to build a home in Shadwell, which is where I grew up, played cricket and football, debated politics, and dreamed about distant shores.

During my high school years, my mother finally decided that the family needed to leave the Caribbean. Like most Caribbean parents, she wanted to give her five children better access to higher education. After overcoming some ambivalence from my father, the family left Saint Kitts when I was seventeen years old.

I got the idea to become a physician because my mom was in health care. She was a district nurse, which is the equivalent of a nurse practitioner today. I remember meeting the physician she worked with when I was about seven or so. He was very impressive—dashing— and was somebody I wanted to emulate. From then on, I told my mother that I wanted to be a doctor.

When I was in Catholic school, the curriculum was weak on science. I told my parents I wanted to leave private school to attend public school. They were kind of upset and worried that I wanted to go there, but they let me go. In the public school, they were doing chemistry, math, and physics—things I knew I needed to learn to become a doctor.

We arrived in Brooklyn in July 1978, a family of seven with a whole bunch of suitcases. It felt like the hottest day of the year. Before arriving in the United States, I had never lived in an apartment.

I started college my first year in the States. My brothers and sisters did well in high school and would go on to schools like MIT, Cornell, and Wellesley. My parents sacrificed a lot so their children could have the best education, and their example has carried over into my marriage and my family in countless ways.

Before I graduated college, I met Joanne, who became my wife. In a year we had our first child, and then came graduate school, followed by medical school, two more children, and my residency in anesthesia.

It may sound cliché, but you have to really like what you do. I'm not really sure that I always liked what I did during the journey to where I am. But I am quite certain that helping people has been a recurring theme in my life. Medicine is an excellent vehicle for making changes and helping other people make changes. I enjoy doing that more than anything else. In my own life, I've made things happen. I enjoy learning.

I have been in positions of leadership, creating systems and policies to help people become better than what they ever thought they could be. I have had the opportunity to train doctors, lead departments, help people develop into what they want to be, and make changes for the better in health care and other areas of medicine. I was part of a team that transitioned from doing only inpatient surgeries to doing ambulatory surgeries, where people would go in and come out the same day. At the time, that was a cutting-edge development in medicine, and I was the first director of ambulatory surgery at SUNY Downstate Medical Center. I viewed it as a way of increasing access to good medical care for people who need it.

Similarly, in my current position at Woodhull Medical Center, I'm working to improve patients' access to surgery. Our area demographic primarily comprises black, Hispanic, and Polish populations—all low income. We have some patients who wait more than thirty days to get access to care; I want to improve on that as well as the efficiency of the operating room, safety, patient satisfaction, and the overall volume of surgeries at this institution. These changes have to happen, especially since Brooklyn is ground zero for health care. Our goal is to make sure the hospital looks good and feels good, that our patients are not in pain, that they refer others, and that we provide the best hospital experience our patients have ever had.

I try to pull people along. I want people to do their best all the time. I've also begun to realize that I've learned a lot from my father about being diplomatic. I listen more; I motivate and coach based on my experiences. With every personality, there is a way to motivate and incentivize. As a leader, you have to find out what is important to a person; you have to really get to know what motivates the members of your team. I do whatever I can to make sure that people understand and focus on our common goal of creating the optimum patient experience. Once they understand the goal, I am like a choreographer, organizing very talented resources to work together, at the same time, always with the same goal in mind. When they do, the results can be remarkable.

In addition to my work here, I feel an obligation to improve life in Saint Kitts. Since 2002, I have been more involved with my homeland, going back more frequently. I was involved with a group called Doctors on Call, composed of colleagues from various hospitals in the city. We were invited to bring surgical services to the island. I started a practice there, specializing in pain management.

Collaborating with the Board of Culture, I would also like to bring more literature and arts events to Saint Kitts. Working together with the board, I think I really can make a difference in the quality of people's lives, not just medically, but culturally, also.

Principle Three

THE CAPTAIN SETS THE COURSE, THE WHOLE CREW PADDLES

When I look back at all the effort I have expended to make something of my life and at all the complex events and experiences that brought me to where I am, I realize how much of my life has been a balancing act: paying careful attention to my own development and realizing how my needs and wants influence and are influenced by others. We all live alongside other individuals and within groups, and there is an art to navigating our way so that we promote and don't stifle one another.

As I've spoken of in earlier chapters, my family life was the greatest influence on me, as it is for us all.

Then there was college and law school, during which I also helped start EDCSPIN. I left the agency at first to work for the Brooklyn district attorney for three years after completing law school. I then became a lobbyist in Albany for another three years while representing organizations for the disabled, and finally came back in 2007 as CEO of the nonprofit I had helped start, where I still am.

These were all organizations within which I had certain roles and responsibilities. Family is intensely personal, but life at a competitive school like Brooklyn Law or in the workplace at EDCSPIN can quickly become similar to being in a family, taking on elements not only of shared joy or purpose but also of jealousy or rivalry. So, when I look back on it, the dynamic of me versus the group or other individuals was always working, at every stage of my development.

When one reflects on this dynamic, questions invariably arise, including these:

⋄ When should I assert myself, and when should I lay back or compromise?

⋄ Can I actually place certain goals higher than myself? Why would I want to?

⋄ How do I balance empowering others versus self-empowerment?

Taken together, these questions are really asking, how can I be the best leader? That's what I want to focus on in this chapter.

A lot of people who know me tell me I got my earliest training within my family. When I first heard that, I would laugh, but today, I happily acknowledge that it is absolutely the truth. Because of my position in the family, I quickly found myself as the leader.

There was no choice, since I was the eldest and my parents were rarely home because of their jobs. I really didn't know anything about being a leader, nor did I think about what the term meant. Instead, my main concern was making sure my brothers and sisters were safe, fed, properly dressed, and attending school.

I was not a leader outside my household; that would come later. However, the lessons I absorbed while helping my siblings carried over into my current position at EDCSPIN. At the agency, I'm responsible for more than 500 employees. I don't have to see that they are fed or properly dressed, although their safety is still important to me. My primary focus is on trying to encourage all of them to work with me toward the goal of helping our clients.

There's no single way to accomplish that; anyone who supervises other people knows this. Different approaches must be used to achieve the same goal. I learned that while trying to convince a sibling to behave: Cajoling worked with one, angry looks with another. I picked up more techniques through trial and error and from imitating others I saw in leadership positions: college administrators, the district attorney, elected officials during my stint as a lobbyist, and now from board members at the agency.

The main point is that I have to accept responsibility as the leader, guiding my staff in both form and context. I have to do what is right and appropriate, which encourages my staff to follow suit. At the same time, I have to conduct myself within ethical and legal standards. If I fall short, I must acknowledge my mistake.

None of this happens in isolation. As I mentioned before, the core values of a leader are based on his or her integrity; namely, that part of an individual that no one knows in detail but that everyone hopes is good, positive, and moral. The core of this integrity depends on trust. When signs of shortcomings are observed, distrust becomes the reality. Top leaders attain enduring success and prominence through professional will and personal humility, all the while understanding that criticism serves as a feedback loop to guide them in achieving still more.

I also learned that leadership doesn't come with days off. Great leaders have a full-time mentality that takes them to a higher level of achievement. Great leaders make a full commitment to their company, organization, school, community, country, and other relevant affiliations. Great leaders are fully engaged.

Another thing I learned is that not everyone can be a leader. Leadership doesn't come just from outside factors; it must also come from within. While we can't all be leaders, we can all be motivated, hardworking, and responsible adults.

The secret is motivation. And I've learned a variety of ways to encourage and motivate my staff.

Praise: A Group Worthy of Loyalty

Recognition and rewards is one area that is often overlooked in organizations. People are expected to do their jobs and to perform to the best of their ability, and while that's the ideal, it's also not reality. Some people naturally work hard and are self-motivated, but many others need a push. Occasional compliments go a long way toward keeping someone focused on her job. After all, everyone needs a pat on the back and a word of praise.

Nothing complicated is required; just send a note or maybe some flowers. That's the underlying theme behind such holidays as Administrative Professionals Day, Boss's Day, and the like. They give an opportunity to thank someone for contributing to the success of the organization. Employee of the Month awards are part of the same process. Good organizations provide these kinds of avenues to recognize and reward employees.

The end result is better, more motivated workers. People who are highly self-motivated may not need a pat on the back, but the rest of us aren't that fortunate. We need encouragement and affirmation to stay positive. Nothing provides a better boost to ego than a compliment. Few of us have such confidence that a compliment has no impact.

In fact, most of us feel like outsiders at one time or another. For example, I felt out of place when I started studying at Lincoln University in Pennsylvania. My parents let me go only because an aunt was attending classes there. The setting was strange, almost alien, because it was rural, not like the big city I was used to. I didn't know anyone, and I really felt inferior. It wasn't that my classmates were smarter, but many came from what appeared to be affluent backgrounds. I couldn't help but feel that they were more sophisticated and experienced than I was. After all, at one point I was commuting 350 miles from my home in Brooklyn to the campus, three days a week, and working the other days simply to pay my tuition and reduce expenses. Life for me in those days was not about spending money, wearing designer clothes, or having a lavish lifestyle.

Little changed when I entered law school. Again, many of my classmates seemed so sure of themselves while I was helping found EDCSPIN, maintaining an internship at night, living independently, and struggling to find the energy to keep up. I knew I was as intelligent as anyone there, but I lacked the broad background my colleagues seemed to have. They fit in; I stood out.

Only later did I realize that they, like me, also felt insecure. We all had to find our place in the world. Sometimes, putting on a mask of confidence helps a person survive until experience creates the real thing. I'd like to think I seemed confident even when I wasn't.

I have never been the type to seek compliments, but during those early days I was very grateful when a professor and, later at the DA's office, a supervisor unexpectedly said nice words about my work. That boosted my confidence and helped me feel that I belonged and had added value. These compliments showed that someone took positive notice of what I was doing. Most of us work hard with little feedback, positive or negative. That doesn't motivate anyone.

In fact, a recent Gallup poll found that among workers who really hate their jobs, 57 percent said they were ignored at work.[1] A timely word of genuine appreciation and admiration could reverse that situation for many people. If no one seems to care if you exist, it's hard for you to concentrate on doing your job to the best of your ability. We all need to feel we are part of the larger company and making a contribution, however small.

At EDCSPIN, I make sure that every employee receives some kind of feedback on a regular basis. They need to know I care. They also need to be aware that I am aware of what they are doing and that their contribution to the success of the agency matters. Through these moments of feedback, they realize I am watching them. That's really motivating, as I know; the agency's board of directors watches me. They, in turn, are watched by state regulators. None of us exists in isolation, like a lone fish in a bowl.

Attention like this builds loyalty. By the way, this is not

a popular approach these days. In fact, in many ways, I am bucking a trend. Companies today have moved away from the model of loyalty to the employee and the employee's loyalty to the organization. No one sticks around to get fifty-year pins anymore. The Japanese were once famous for "cradle to grave" employment—not anymore. Few businesses follow that approach. It's just too expensive to continually give raises and boost benefits. Companies now typically hire workers for limited projects and then jettison them.

I'm reminded of a *Doonesbury* cartoon where a boss tells a colleague that he intends to fire everyone and hire them back as contract employees. He cites the millions in savings. His colleague bubbles enthusiastically over the idea and suggests that "we" could really boost the bottom line.

The boss turns to his colleague and says simply, "We?"

The "everyone is replaceable" syndrome undermines loyalty. It may be a necessary business model in certain conditions, but it's hardly motivating. Compliments go a long way to reduce the fear and ease the pain of such an approach, and so does the addition of perks—an assigned parking spot, coupons for meals, or other simple incentives. Such initiatives should not be undertaken in a cynical effort to manipulate, but rather as a sincere effort to reward employees deserving of recognition. Empty compliments are quickly recognized and can reduce motivation. Large recognitions like raises are always welcome, but even a small gesture is greatly appreciated.

Fair Treatment: Our Work Is About Others

When I was in college, I expected to be treated fairly, no matter how I was dressed or looked. Many times I arrived in class looking unorganized, arriving straight from an impromptu stay at a friend's apartment or from a long commute, but professors did not seem to notice. I would have been upset if they had. Fairness is part of American culture. We Americans do not like it when people cut in line ahead of us to join a friend or seem to take an unfair advantage. We expect everyone to be treated the same. The idea is enshrined in the Declaration of Independence: "All men are created equal."

It took this country a while for the concept to achieve reality. As we all know, slavery ensured that a portion of society was definitely not equal. Women, too, had to fight for their rights, right along with the disabled and gay members of the American family. Those battles continue, although we are definitely closer to achieving equality in many areas.

But those changes came from attitude as well as legislation. The 1964 Civil Rights Act and other national laws helped guarantee the backing of legal authorities if discrimination occurs. At the same time, the emergence of popular black, gay, and disabled athletes, movie actors, political figures, and other leaders has helped ease the stigmas such persons often confront.

For me, this has meant that I have not run into many of

the same harsh barriers faced by my grandparents and parents. Prejudice still exists and probably always will among some elements of society. Nevertheless, it's not as daunting. With my law degree, for example, I was given the opportunity to pass or fail on my own.

That same concept of equality has to be part of an organization. People have to see that they have a chance to achieve promotions, raises, and other symbols of success based on merit and not on connections or whims. That's reflected in the rewards, as I mentioned in the previous section. Distribution of awards and prizes must be seen as fair in order for them to have any effect or meaning. Bosses who reward only their "pets" quickly generate resentment. Without question, favoritism undermines everything any organization is trying to achieve.

Admittedly, fairness is not perfect. There are a few positions that cannot be available to everyone. For example, a disabled person might have problems with the physical demands of being a firefighter, but there's no reason someone in a wheelchair can't work on the administrative side of that career.

The more an organization looks to merit as a reward criterion, the more employees will work to demonstrate that they deserve such recognition. People who do not feel they have an opportunity because of extraneous conditions quickly lose their motivation for hard work. Fairness also requires that each employee have specific and measurable responsibilities.

I can't criticize a faulty effort if a worker doesn't know what he was supposed to do in the first place.

Placement: Workers Aligned Properly

I strongly believe that anyone who can help another should see it as a privilege and should answer that call. That's why I cofounded EDCSPIN and eventually became its CEO. This turned out to be the right place for me.

We all need to find the best vehicle for our skills and interests. A manager's responsibility is to put an employee in a place where he can achieve the best results.

I don't hire a ballerina to fix the plumbing, for example. If I need someone to use an oar properly, I don't look for someone who knows only how to build a boat. As an attorney, I found that my forte was in developing strategy and arguing in court, not gathering information. The district attorney recognized where my talents lay and allowed me to shine in the area I was strongest.

I take that same approach with my agency. Some people might not be good social workers. They may not enjoy working with clients or have the patience necessary to aid disabled clients with severe needs. However, they may be superb at arranging for treatment and identifying resources. They can be vital members of a team by contributing where they can help the most and achieve personal satisfaction at the same time.

And after all, the alternative isn't pretty. Employees who are misplaced can burn out, get bored, or resent being forced to learn a job they have no interest in.

The process has to begin with interviewing. People regularly apply for positions they are not qualified for simply because they need a job or because they think the opening sounds interesting. But here are some things to look for to make sure that the people you hire are really the best fit for the position:

- ◇ The candidate doesn't know key terms or information he or she should know, based on previous experiences.
- ◇ The candidate supplies references that are not former employers but colleagues.
- ◇ The candidate talks in generalities rather than specifics related to prior job experiences.

To increase our chances of choosing the right candidate, I developed a checklist of what I want the ideal candidate to be able to do. I set the standards for minimal qualifications. That narrows down the list of possible candidates because a large agency like EDCSPIN can have hundreds of applicants for one opening. I want to be sure only the best-qualified candidates actually get into my office for an interview.

I conduct very thorough interviews. I'm looking not only at qualifications and ability but also at whether the candidate fits into the agency's culture. That's more important than many people realize. A brusque person, for example, may cause dissension in an agency where people are considerate of one another.

If I am thorough, I may find someone ill suited for the position she applied for but perfect for another position she had not considered. My goal is to have the best employees working together toward a common goal, paddling together in the same direction, toward the same destination. That's all.

Some companies actually move employees around on a regular basis in hopes of finding the ideal landing spot. Brown & Brown, a large insurance company, employs that strategy. Apparently it works; the company continues to grow.

Handle Complaints: Listen to Everybody

Every now and then one of my brothers and sisters would grumble to me about something. They expected me to respond. Personally, I don't like complaining, but I gradually began to understand why my siblings chose that method of expression. They had concerns and, occasionally, objections. Without a valid route to express their concerns, they groused. Many times they got what they wanted because I—and probably most people—really dislike listening to complaints.

Their grumbling came naturally, as it turns out. Dr. Charles Smith, a Kansas State University professor who specializes in parent-child relationships, says that whining is instilled in childhood: "Children whine because they have learned that kind of repetitious, aggravating behavior gets them what they want. Parents have to realize they created this behavior and now they're going to have to suffer through it."[2] Those of us in the same boat have to suffer as well.

My employees are no different from my siblings in this regard. They are real people who occasionally don't like what they are seeing or are forced to do for their job, and as a result they start complaining. Having seen and heard my share of complainers, I have learned some ways to deal with them that don't include abject surrender in frustration. I'm not suggesting that my approach will work for everyone who grouses, but it has certainly helped at EDCSPIN. Not surprisingly, the same method can work with employees who have unpleasant attitudes.

- ◇ *Don't waste time listening.* I am the boss, so I can say I'm not interested. Colleagues of a constant complainer just need to politely excuse themselves. Complainers abhor silence. They want to vent, and they need an audience for that.
- ◇ *Give credit.* People may grumble because they are looking for attention. They don't necessarily want a raise, but, as noted earlier, employees love recognition for quality work. This isn't a case of the

"squeaky wheel getting the grease," but, as noted
earlier, a need for real recognition for a strong effort.

◇ *Make sure an employee knows his future possibilities*
within the company. Employees need to understand
what the company goals are and why certain actions
were taken to align with those goals. They can see
what part they play and how their actions affect
others. That tends to reduce whining and increase
focus.

◇ *Good communication is always significant.* I'll expand
on the critical need for good communication in the
next chapter.

◇ *When the complaint is job related, try understanding*
what the concern is really about. There actually may be
something of value behind the grousing. Employees
may be reluctant to approach their supervisor or
put an objection in writing. Sometimes, a simple
explanation will suffice to stifle a grumble. I often
hold group meetings to provide explanations for
decisions, acknowledging when there are concerns.
A side benefit is that employees may raise good
points or propose modifications that improve
the original idea. I never hesitate to encourage
employees to offer their suggestions or to accept
those that are plausible or doable. Then, employees

want the plan to succeed as much as I do.

◇ *Use humor if possible.* Music may or may not calm the savage beast, but humor can certainly counter bad attitudes. It can be injected through informal discussions.

Remember not to stereotype people who constantly complain. Complainers come in all shapes and sizes. As a result, they cannot all be silenced the same way. For example, some make excuses for everything. To counter them, don't allow excuses. That was the policy in law school. It didn't matter why an assignment was submitted late. After all, courts set deadlines, and those deadlines have to be met. That's true on any job. This way, employees learn to let a supervisor know when there is a problem that may cause a delay. That opens communication channels often blocked by whining.

I doubt that grousing can be completely eliminated. Even the best, most motivated employees may find something they don't like. On the other hand, some people just complain about everything. A company needs to provide avenues through which all employees may raise concerns without recrimination. For people who automatically say no, the response is similar: Ask them for their suggestions and ideas. It's easy to complain; it's harder to provide alternatives. As a result, I often tell my staff: "Don't bring me the problem—bring me the solution."

I also attack complaining from another perspective. I try to eliminate the reasons for the grumbles. This is a multi-step process.

1. *Every employee gets a clear definition of his or her job requirements.* Each of my social workers knows how many hours she is expected to work and other aspects of her job. She knows this before she is offered the job. That helps curtail complaints, since elements of any job can be difficult or annoying. Employees know what is expected; therefore, there's no reason to complain. Besides, if an employee can come up with a better way to do her job, I'm ready to listen.

2. *Each employee knows precisely what he or she is accountable for.* Every time she visits a client, she must turn in a report. There are regular meetings with supervisors to discuss progress, problems, and plans. The lines of communication remain open so that any problems are addressed before the employee turns to grumbling in order to be heard.

3. *Adopt an open-door/open-discussion policy.* Employees are not punished for coming to see me about a concern. I always include their supervisor in any decision. As a result, everyone is welcomed and stays on the same page. This started when I

arrived in 2007. Some members of the previous administration did not allow the free flow of information from the staff to the director and back. Oftentimes, it was a one-way street. Unfortunately, that often led to information traffic jams, confusion, and unproductivity.

4. *Address employee concerns; each person is naturally concerned first and foremost about him- or herself.* Regardless of how petty a complaint may seem, it's not petty to the employee who raised it. For example, when we needed to replace the carpet in the agency, employees at all levels were involved in picking the color and even the style. This is called a "buy-in." The employees bought into the process because they were part of it.

5. *Reduce stress.* This is a really serious problem in American business, where 90 percent of employees complain about excess stress. Much of that comes from their feeling of a lack of control over their circumstances. The best answer is to get employees involved not just in decisions but also in understanding the direction the company wants to go and why.

As with most things, clear and open communication reduces complaints, leaving grumblers with nothing to moan about. Often, though, the complaints really aren't about a boss or some element of the job. Instead, the problem may be the job itself. After all, some people were not cut out to use an oar, but would make great navigators or coxswains. As noted earlier, the key is to put people where they can use their natural abilities to the organization's greatest advantage.

Setting a Good Example: Leadership Without Leaders

Throughout my life, I have enjoyed performing in track-and-field events. Today, I go skydiving and compete in marathons. I don't just tell employees to try to stay in shape and keep active; I actually do something about it by practicing what I preach.

I also want my employees to see how we must work together by having them participate in agency decisions. For me, this embodies what Dr. King meant when he said, "Leadership and followership go hand in hand." The civil rights icon also used to say that a genuine leader is not a searcher for consensus but a molder of consensus.

It takes a person of great integrity and perseverance to see what is needed in society and decide to lead change. As Dr. King said, "If we are to go forward, we must go back and rediscover those precious values—that all reality hinges on moral foundations and that all reality has spiritual control."[3]

I believe I am succeeding. A nonprofit developer once said

that I am a "thought-provoking visionary who speaks from his experience and humble beginnings that have allowed him to be a firm yet compassionate leader who sets an example for those around him." That example is about dedication, commitment, and hard work. I am in my office early in the morning and on weekends, and I stay late. If I expect my staff to give their all, I must be willing to do the same. EDCSPIN employees can't miss that model.

Anyone in a leadership position can do the same thing.

◆　◆　◆

Throughout my career, I have come across people whose experiences have empowered and inspired me. Stacie Henderson is one of those people. So, I decided to write her story because it must be told; extraordinary people's experiences are worth knowing. Her commitment to excellence explains her rise to prominence in the intensely competitive world of high-fashion marketing and retail. Her experience illuminates the ways that a gifted, self-aware leader can focus a team's efforts to achieve lofty goals in a high-pressure environment, then refocus and recalibrate those same abilities to move a new team in an entirely new direction.

PERSPECTIVE: STACIE HENDERSON—TIRELESS VISIONARY

Charles A. Archer

The "Everybody Paddles" mission is meant to inspire people to work at the same time, in the same direction, toward the same goal. The mission requires a team effort and implies that no one can be left behind. But what happens when those goals have been attained, when there is seemingly nowhere left to paddle? Sometimes we may believe that this point has been reached—until an immense opportunity presents itself.

Take Stacie Henderson's experience, for example. She is the quintessential polished professional. Soon after obtaining a master's degree in fashion management from SDA Bocconi (a Triple Crown Business School), she focused her talents on creative marketing strategies for the luxury brand Salvatore Ferragamo SPA in Florence, Italy. Before she was able to truly fulfill her role there, she had to acquaint herself with the Italian culture. After becoming fluent both linguistically and culturally, Henderson strengthened the Ferragamo Parfums fragrance portfolio in the Japanese market by overseeing the strategic marketing of a new fragrance, Incanto Dream. The success of her strategy resulted in the global rollout of the fragrance. Henderson's dedication and vision for the brand led her to the position of global marketing director. With a wealth of experience and a firm grasp on consumer-trends research, Henderson decided it was time to paddle forward.

In February 2006, Henderson returned to the United States and began a new role as director of marketing for the international luxury brand Versace in New York City. Wasting no time, she developed marketing programs that targeted micro-segmentation of potential customers, aggressive product-focused media plans, and vital collaborations with key organizations. As a part of the executive team, Henderson developed marketing strategies that supported sales for both the retail and the wholesale divisions. She was part of a dynamic executive team that witnessed double-digit growth for the brand. Henderson continued her eminence and sharpened her focus by implementing social media and email marketing strategies to enhance Versace's global presence, which brought about a triple-digit database increase. Her dedication, drive, and fearlessness in taking the plunge into digital efforts with Versace played an instrumental role in her promotion to vice president of marketing and events.

With all of these achievements and a solid international network of high-end fashion industry professionals, what more could she have wanted? During a recent interview, she spoke candidly about her time at Versace.

"I loved everything about my job. There was nothing about it that I disliked, but I knew that I wanted something that would challenge me, constantly . . . I realized that sometimes you have to take a chance and try something new that provides you a new set of challenges. I still keep in touch with my Versace family. I learned so much from my time there."

Henderson found her new set of challenges when she was contacted regarding a position with the U.S. unit of the Westfield Group as vice president of marketing for the Westfield World Trade Center. "When I was told that I had the opportunity to be instrumental in changing the landscape of downtown Lower Manhattan," she said, "I realized this was a pretty big deal."

Westfield oversees retail operations for a 350,000-square-foot shopping and dining complex at the World Trade Center site. This is the first New York City undertaking for Westfield, which initially acquired the rights to the WTC retail complex in 2001. Adding this latest enhancement to its global retail real estate portfolio, Westfield has designed a space that will hold 150 shops (fashion, dining, services, and others), and Stacie Henderson manages the brand positioning, advertising, digital outreach, public relations, and tourism for the new retail district.

And Henderson's vision is broader than the formidable business opportunities involved in the undertaking. "The beauty is, we are looking at this as the rebirth, the revitalization of this area." As an integral part of the Westfield team, Henderson has already started the process of creating the tightest possible focus for her target consumer audience. Her primary objective is to work with her team to create a destination that will top the must-see lists of New Yorkers and visitors alike.

Henderson is steadfast in her vision for this retail space. While recognizing that rebuilding downtown Manhattan is a huge endeavor, she is sure that the team she has become a part of will paddle in the same direction, unified in their goal to make this all possible. As she asserts: "It is truly a collective undertaking, and my company is a part of it. There are several organizations that will come together to make this project instrumental to the revival of downtown Manhattan . . . If people walk in and we can surprise and delight them the moment they come through the door—if we can exceed their expectations and give them a great experience—my vision for this space will be fulfilled."

Principle Four

COMMUNICATE CLEARLY TO STAY ON COURSE

~~~

I learned in dramatic fashion about the importance to leaders of clear communication. By the time I was working as a lobbyist in Albany, New York, in 2007, I had taken several courses in communication, through which I learned all the appropriate theories. But as I continued my work within the legislative process to obtain funds for social service agencies around the state, I soon discovered that the theory and the practice of communication were drastically different undertakings.

At that time, I was also on the board of EDCSPIN. Since I lived far away in Albany, my role at the nonprofit was limited to reviewing decisions made by the executive director, approving grants, and the like. When I could be on-site, I also enjoyed providing some input into the agency through mentoring, team-building exercises, training in presentation techniques, as well as modeling professional etiquette.

Imagine my dismay, then, to learn that there were major problems at EDCSPIN. I was stunned and disappointed. On top of that, because of my experience as a lobbyist in the state capital, I was asked to take the reins of our social service agency.

I was hesitant. For one thing, the current executive director was very popular, as I saw during my infrequent visits to the agency. The staff liked him, and they were not going to be happy he was leaving. Then, too, I knew that some would speculate that I, as a founding board member, had somehow orchestrated his exit. Any change in leadership excites similar imaginary motives and generates conspiracy theories. Finally, there was the problem of getting the employees to focus on our clients, not on internal personnel matters.

Thus, I was faced with a real communication problem with multiple facets. After a lot of thinking and discussions with friends, I decided to take the job. I then spent a lot of time working out a communication strategy. I needed to calm the staff while, at the same time, maintaining their loyalty to the agency. I also had to ease any concerns our clients might have had and at the same time convince regulatory agencies that EDCSPIN was back on track.

I had little experience dealing with this kind of an emergency. It wasn't like finding a Band-Aid for an injured sibling or figuring out how to come up with the money for tuition. I had handled those problems my entire life. This problem cut across so many more boundaries than anything I had faced before.

Large corporations often hire public relations companies that provide guidance during testing times in an organization's life. I didn't have that luxury. Besides, adding an outsider to the mix would only have increased confusion. I needed to show that I was in charge and could handle the complex situation. What I said mattered; how I appeared mattered even more. As I will discuss in more detail a bit later, many times tacit communication can be just as important as anything spoken or written.

In this situation, success depended on combining each element to win over a skeptical staff. I could not be afraid to fail. At other points in my life I had failed, but I knew that the secret in such circumstances is to get back up, brush off the "dust" of a sense of failure or humiliation, and keep trying, just as that great tune "Pick Yourself Up" put it so well.[1]

Opening Act: Creating Positive First Impressions

I started by sending email announcements to all staff members requiring them to attend a group meeting the day after the former executive director was scheduled to leave. I also had signs posted on the entrance to announce the meeting. I did not tell anyone what the meeting concerned. After all, grapevines have a way of divulging all the news anyway. I scheduled the meeting before normal working hours to be sure our clients were not shortchanged.

On the day of the meeting, I arrived early. I had purchased donuts on the way to work and waited in my office while employees slowly began to arrive. At the time, the agency was in smaller quarters, so there was only one room big enough for everyone to gather in. Everyone gathered in the main room, which included desks and chairs as well as a coffee machine.

I didn't have to be with them long to know that they were turning on the whine engine full blast. Some employees were "sure" I had engineered a takeover. Others were equally "sure" that the previous director should not have been let go. Everyone traded rumors, ratcheting up emotions along the way.

I did not interfere.

About fifteen minutes before the scheduled meeting, I walked into the room and set out the donuts. I didn't say anything, but I wanted the employees to know I cared about them and about not wasting money, so these weren't fancy. The former executive director used to put out any pastries left over from his meetings, so employees knew what the directors were served; the difference was obvious.

No one spoke to me, although they flocked to the donuts with obvious enthusiasm. Next time, I decided, I'd opt for a healthier snack.

At the exact time set for the meeting, I walked forward and stood in front of the group. Eyes followed me from the moment I stepped through the doorway. Everyone grew quiet. I could sense hostility. Most did not know me. I may have been cofounder of the agency, but I had worked in another city. The board meetings were held after-hours. I recognized only a few faces.

I had left my tie and suit coat in the office. My intent was to demonstrate again without saying anything that I was a working person like them and that I was rolling up my sleeves too. I didn't have to ask for quiet; side conversations had stopped, and everyone was staring at me. I stood in front of them for a moment, calmly counting heads. The pause gave me time to relax. It also allowed them to look at me and register my appearance. The previous director had his own, very individual style that set him off from everyone else. In contrast, my style is to dress like the staff. They knew immediately that things were very different, even before I said anything.

Most of the staffers sat in small clumps, where they had been whispering to one another. Everyone seemed to have a cup of coffee and a donut; the three boxes in the back of the room were already empty.

I smiled. I really can't claim to be personable; my intent was not to make friends, but rather to show that they had a strong leader who was not intimidated by the needs of the moment. They needed to recognize that their jobs were safe and that the agency would not be closing. The calmer I was, the calmer they would be. So, I smiled, and after a moment, I could almost see people relaxing. I knew I had to sound strong, not scared or shaky. Employees would read trouble into my words if they were not clear and confident. I wanted to communicate all of this with my demeanor.

I could almost hear the many questions bubbling just below the surface of the faces watching me. Since I hadn't intended to become the executive director, I had prepared no speech. Instead, I decided to speak from the heart.

"Some of you know me," I said quietly. I did not shout. "For the rest, let me introduce myself. More than a decade ago, I helped start this agency. Some of you know I have been on the board of directors." I paused. Everyone continued to stare. "As of today, I am your chief executive officer." I spoke in a straightforward manner, without a hint that the announcement was anything special.

I could hear the whispers start. Everyone wanted to know what had happened. I did not tell them; that was none of their business. Instead, I assured them that the agency would continue normally. Their positions would be unaffected. I told them that the agency would open its doors at the usual time, and they would resume helping our clients as always. Naturally, that prompted other questions. I answered each one patiently. I was honest, but there were things they did not need to know. I believe strongly in providing the information that employees must have, but that doesn't mean they need every detail. Besides, such nonessential information often gets distorted in the retelling and creates more problems.

Employees learned that their salaries would not drop and that positions would not be affected unless someone was not qualified for the job. I knew—as did everyone else—that the previous director had hired a few friends. They resigned shortly thereafter, which relieved me of the need to fire them. At the first meeting, employees also learned that the state had complete confidence in the agency's ability to fulfill its contracts, and that I did too. They learned that I planned no major changes; that the agency had a strong future; that they were important; and that I cared about their futures. Some of this message was stated; the rest came through in how I spoke and was communicated by my firm, upright stance. They could tell I meant everything I said.

The whole meeting lasted less than fifteen minutes. I deliberately did not leave a lot of time between the end of it and when the agency usually opened. I knew that the staff would get antsy, eager to not fall behind on the work schedule. Thus, in effect, they managed themselves. Besides, not many would have the nerve to speak up at a large meeting. Consequently, I also scheduled a one-on-one meeting with each employee as well as additional group sessions.

I used the large gatherings to stress teamwork. Initially, I relied on the "We are in the same boat" metaphor, and that soon expanded into the "Everybody Paddles" concept.

Meetings with individuals were as short or as long as the person required. Some people wanted to talk; this was not so much to find answers as to ingratiate themselves with me. That did not cloud my judgment. I looked at what they were doing, not how manipulative they were acting.

A few were in positions they were not qualified for. Because they were good workers, however, I was able to shift people around to better match skills to positions. I also needed to demonstrate flexibility. The employees had to know I was not a dictator, that I was a partner in the agency's efforts. I was picking up my paddle, too.

Some of the individual meetings were difficult, to be sure. Several staffers had been hired by the previous director and were very loyal to him. I needed for them to transfer that loyalty to me, and that could happen only with one-on-one conversations where they could see and hear that I shared their enthusiasm for their work and actually knew a lot about it. At the same time, they had to know they did not face any kind of punishment for supporting their former boss. Confidence and knowledge communicate their own strong messages.

Virtually all of those employees wanted to stay and soon began to trust my leadership. But not everyone chose to remain, and when that happened, I understood. Some people were committed to the previous director, and nothing I said or did could change that. I did not reprimand them; I sympathized with their need to make such a life-changing decision and wished them well.

I also tried to help them find new jobs. Because of my lobbying experience, I knew directors at other agencies and was able to locate positions suited to the abilities of some former EDCSPIN employees. Admittedly, I was not unhappy to see them leave, since I knew that the new people I hired would be concerned about pleasing me, not trying to undermine whatever I chose to do.

The most important aspect was to maintain open communication. Employers must communicate often, especially with each other. Alex "Sandy" Pentland, the director of MIT's Human Dynamics Laboratory and the MIT Media Lab Entrepreneurship Program, said that in a "typical project team, a dozen or so communication exchanges per working hour may turn out to be optimum; but more or less than that, and team performance can decline."[2]

Such communication can be broken into three types: tacit, oral, and written. Each type of communication plays an important role in any successful organization.

Tacit: Nonverbal Behavior

As you could see in the scenario I described above, I sent nonverbal messages through such visual cues as the donuts, my clothing, and my manner when standing in front of the employees. My efforts seemed effective, and certainly that approach was better than a written manifesto or some other document.

Dr. Mehmet Oz, a cardiac surgeon and TV guru, says that silent communication methods "are more powerful than we give them credit for. At times, they speak volumes. Far more than even a multitude of words can. What we portray visually, through how we dress, the manner in which we carry ourselves, our nonverbal communiqués—this all sends messages to those around us."[3]

Those messages are important. I've quoted one of my role models several times already, and here, too, I believe Dr. Martin Luther King Jr. provided the best example of using tacit communication that I can think of. When he spoke, he spoke directly and honestly. While his words were important, his audience could see by his manner, even without his words, that he lived what he was saying and would continue to live it after he left the podium or stage. When King stepped in front of an audience, he seemed to electrify everyone there. That connection created an experience rather than simply an event. People tuned in to one another as well as to Dr. King. They were moved to action simply by his presence. I don't want to suggest that everyone has that kind of charisma, but any leader must be aware of the energy of his or her audience and tap into it.

Perhaps the most-studied form of nonverbal communication involves body language. I was well aware of that and made sure that at the initial staff meeting I stood as tall as I could, with my body facing my audience. I'm not a tall person, but thin pants and a straight back help create an illusion of height. When I was asked a question, I turned to face the person asking and answered directly without pause. I kept my hands out of my pockets and tried to present a picture of control.

I wasn't doing anything new. The ancient Greeks understood that how we stand and look displays information, and scholars in the 1600s wrote treatises on hand gestures. In the mid-nineteenth century, evolutionary theorist Charles Darwin also studied body language, yet most people were unaware of the topic until the publication in 1970 of *Body Language* by Julius Fast.

Today there are lists that "decode" body language. For example, frequent blinking denotes excitement or pressure. Biting lips indicates pressure, while tilting your head to the side demonstrates submission and/or thoughtfulness. On a closer level, dilated eyes show interest and curiosity.[4]

For most of us, the signs are obvious. We get most of our information about the world through our eyes and so are constantly "reading" the appearance of the people around us. The secret for a successful speaker involves being aware of the messages that listeners are sending subliminally. At my first meeting as executive director, for example, some staffers stood erect, with arms folded across their chests. That's clearly a defensive, defiant gesture. People leaning forward were indicating interest.

I always try to be aware of the basic body signals of others. People perform them unconsciously, giving a careful observer hints into their inner thoughts. Everything matters: where people sit in relation to one another; what they sit on; and how they are arranged with respect to the furniture and setting. This is true for a large gathering or a private meeting.

As a result, I arranged the chairs in my office for the one-on-one sessions so that the employee did not sit directly across from me with my desk separating us. That positioning can seem confrontational or intimidating. Instead, I moved the chair to the side of the desk. That way, the employee was almost on a level with me. The chair also was not placed against the desk, but a few inches back. That provided some private space for the employee. Too close, and a person feels crowded; too far away, and it's much harder to create feelings of trust.

I also leaned back and relaxed as I spoke with employees. Each person who came to my office for a meeting was offered a piece of candy. My opening was pleasant: a cheery welcome, a handshake. I did everything I could to make the employee feel comfortable despite being called into the office the way a student may be hauled into a principal's office at school. We all dreaded that, even if we hadn't done anything wrong. A big smile and candy helped allay fears.

I knew each staffer would initially feel uncomfortable, so I tried to help them relax. I answered questions honestly and listened to them. I did care what they were thinking, but they could know that only if I focused on them while they talked. If I fiddled with a pen or checked out paperwork, they could get the message that I did not care. Instead, each employee got my undivided attention.

Such efforts really paid off. The agency quickly recovered its balance. We found some solid new employees to replace those who left.

But part of that success was also due to oral communication.

Oral: Choose Your Words Wisely

Just as how I appeared to the employees was important, so was what I said. That includes everything from tone to word choice.

I began my initial meeting at EDCSPIN (just as I've begun these types of meetings ever since) by analyzing my audience. I recognized that I would be talking to an educated group of employees: social workers, all of whom had college degrees. Many came from highly rated universities. In some ways these meetings were akin to my first few days at Lincoln University, where I was acutely aware of how better prepared the other students were. In this case, however, I was older and more experienced, and I held a law degree from a fine university. As a result, I could talk to employees on their level.

That was very important. We've all heard people who use big words and try to impress listeners with their vocabulary. I wasn't trying to wow anyone. I just wanted to be sure to communicate my intentions.

As with all presentations, I started with the basic question: What did my audience need to know? Staffers at EDCSPIN needed to be aware that there had been a change in leadership, but that their income and careers were not affected. People are always interested in the impact of change on their lives. They wanted to know what would happen next; I told them. They wanted their questions answered; I did that too. I spoke clearly, but I did not raise my voice, which would have implied that I was dictating to them. I also didn't whisper, which could denote fear. After all, we were in a large room, and I needed the people in the back to hear what I said and not have to ask someone nearby for a translation.

I tried to be natural; I was talking with my colleagues, not lecturing. As in all speeches, I stressed the key points, which meant reminding everyone at the conclusion about what was going to be the next step—individual meetings.

I also tried to look at everyone, but not for a long time at any single person. People can get intimidated if a speaker focuses on them. However, by looking around the room, I included everyone in the process.

My tone of voice was also a very deliberate choice. It's possible to say the same thing with inflections that change the meaning. Think of the first words I said: "Some of you know me. For the rest, let me introduce myself. More than a decade ago, I helped start this agency. Some of you know I have been on the board of directors. As of today, I am your chief executive officer."

If I had said those first words in a haughty manner, I would have turned off the staff. If I had said them in a defiant way, I could have set up a confrontation. Instead, I was conversational. I established my credentials as one of the agency's founders and then emphasized the main point. I emphasized my new status by smiling. The silent message enhanced the spoken one.

I made sure the message was on target, clear, and brief. We've all heard people talk too long, like ministers at church who forget to end their sermon.

None of this happened by accident. I had to think about my message. When I first began working, I didn't have these skills. Today I am confident in my ability to speak before any group. That confidence came from practice, teaching as an adjunct professor at Baruch College, and lecturing on behalf of the American Association on Intellectual and Developmental Disabilities, along with speaking to various audiences throughout the region. Control of one's tone is like any other skill; it improves with practice.

Written: Redraft the Script

The oral presentation went well, but it had to be reinforced. That's where writing came in. Written communication allowed me to continue the effort to gain the staff's support even when I could not be present.

Even the sign posted for the first meeting was consciously part of that effort. It was typed and printed. It looked professional. It had only the necessary words: "Staff Meeting 8:45 a.m. Tuesday." That was all.

The email to the staff was equally brief and to the point: "Please contact me to set up a meeting to discuss how we can work together to continue the work of EDCSPIN."

Nothing in the notes was threatening. At the same time, the wording clearly stated the objective of the meeting.

Good written communication is vital. For starters, everything written can potentially become a legal document. With written communication, we can trace services given to a client and the progress of a particular case. Such records are both permanent and proof of our efforts that can be provided to regulatory agencies and funding bodies.

At the same time, written communication must be clear or it can create confusion. This is especially true since there's no chance for immediate feedback. I could tell how people felt during my nonverbal and oral communication from their reactions during my brief orientation and in our private sessions, but I didn't see how people reacted to their email.

Written communication does, however, allow for a consistent message. That's evident from the EDCSPIN website, which includes pictures of families with the repeated message that all of us are important and everyone has to work together. The images are pleasant, the colors pastel. The pages exude a sense of peace and enjoyment. Our website also highlights the agency's values: integrity, respect, opportunity, accountability, and togetherness.

Our main message is the focus on togetherness. That idea is emphasized in the "About Us" section: "We consider it a privilege to serve our communities and we are proud of how much has been accomplished in our first two decades. The difference we have made in so many lives could only have been accomplished through the extraordinary effort of a dedicated staff working together."

The concept is also featured in my biography on the website: "Charles Archer firmly believes that 'Everybody is required for Everything!' and he's more than willing to do his part."

If I said that repeatedly, everyone would be bored. However, the idea can be presented in many ways in writing, providing a clear image of what the agency thinks is important. The same theme is picked up on EverybodyPaddles.com, which has a quote from me on the front page: "Everybody paddles . . . at the same time, in the same direction, toward the same goal."

Written communication has two key components: grammar and clarity. The writing must be grammatically correct. I like to think of grammar as a code that everyone knows and follows. Nothing can cause confusion faster than changing the code. It makes things very difficult to understand.

Jesus ran into the problem of changing the code with his parables. Not everyone could understand because he was presenting information in an unfamiliar way. The meanings became clear only after much study, explanation, and understanding.

The same cannot be said, however, for written communication replete with major grammatical or spelling errors. Instead, the reader gets an unwritten message that the writer was careless, uninterested, and possibly illiterate. Few of us will glean anything useful from that kind of writing, nor will we respect the person who produced it.

At the same time, word choice and tone must be appropriate for the audience. Just as with an oral presentation, written communication must be directed at and appropriate for the intended audience.

Business leaders all recognize this. Gilbert Amelio, former president and CEO of National Semiconductor Corporation, spoke for many executives when he said: "Developing excellent communication skills is absolutely essential to effective leadership. The leader must be able to share knowledge and ideas to transmit a sense of urgency and enthusiasm to others. If a leader can't get a message across clearly and motivate others to act on it, then having a message doesn't even matter."[5]

Scott Barkin, a colleague, friend, and executive director at Block Institute, also spoke about the need for united action: "Our job is to get everyone to row in the same direction."

I couldn't have said it better.

◆ ◆ ◆

Christian A. Paul, a banking executive from Saint Lucia, has Caribbean-wide leadership experience. In his "Perspective" essay, he contributes his thoughts on that leadership and on the value of cooperation. As you will see, he is a skilled practitioner of the art of effective leadership communication.

PERSPECTIVE: EQUIP THEM WITH PADDLES

Christian A. Paul

In December 1997 I was appointed country manager of the Anguilla branch of an international bank. I was hired by the bank's regional director at its regional head office in Barbados, where I worked at the time. I felt like I was eight feet tall. After all, I was thirty-two years old, one of the younger managers to hold such a position.

Yes, I felt very proud, and I felt that I deserved it because of my experience and also because I put everything I had into my work.

So, one month later, I was on a flight to Anguilla, ready to change the world! But as I arrived at my new work location, I was unprepared for what I saw. The building looked dilapidated, with moss growing on its faded walls. Were it not for the bank's unmistakable logo on the walls, I would have thought that the taxi had taken me to the wrong place. Nevertheless, I settled in at my hotel with eager anticipation. After all, as my uncle Roger would always say, "A coat of paint can hide a multitude of sins," and surely that's all it would take to get the place looking spick-and-span—or so I thought.

The next morning, all decked out and spiffy, I arrived at the bank. If I wasn't prepared for the state of the building the day before, I would never have been prepared by what I found inside: broken tiles, dated countertops, shabby furniture, and old boxes. The place resembled an old warehouse, and the staff didn't present much better in terms of demeanor.

Who could blame them? They had taken on the character of their surroundings. In short, the ship of my career was heading toward an iceberg, and it was going to be difficult to negotiate a safe course. By this time, my exaggerated sense of stature had quickly returned to my normal 5 feet 9 inches, and my shoulders slumped under the weight of the dreary surroundings.

In the weeks that followed, I learned of the promises by two previous managers to repair the building. This explained why the staff had laughed when, at my first meeting, I said I was going to effect renovations to the building. The employees there were not even in the same boat, much less having paddles.

I decided right there and then that if I was going to have any chance of leading this business with this team, I needed to communicate that change was possible by tackling the physical environment. I reasoned that the condition of the building impacted not only staff morale but also performance.

Armed with little more than instinct and my life experiences thus far, I went about making plans and soliciting assistance from the head office. The original budgets for the renovations took account only of the customer areas, because the staff areas were in good condition at the time. However, the eight years that had elapsed since then had taken a toll on these areas as well. I took a stance: We either renovated everywhere or nowhere. That became my singular focus: First fix the boat that was leaking, and then get the staff on board.

My gamble paid off, and we got things going. We renovated the building, changed furniture, and got staff new uniforms. The boat had been fixed, and it was time to start the journey of repositioning the business, but I still needed people on board to help me get where I wanted to go.

I began by refocusing on earlier initiatives to create a sustained sales and customer service culture. Refurbishing the premises and physical amenities had given us a start, and the staff became gradually more receptive to the various strategies and initiatives to regain a foothold in the market and start growing the business. They began to want to go on the journey, and as we painted a picture of what success would look like, they began to see our destination more clearly. The other, equally important catalyst was reassuring them that we would be doing this together. I had built a massive amount of credibility by delivering on the promise I made when I first arrived, and that credibility earned me the right to ask them to journey with me.

This time I set about creating a high-energy environment. Businesses on the island engaged one another in friendly competition in different sporting disciplines, and we participated in those games. I also included all staff (from messenger to senior supervisor—all seventeen of them) at the annual cocktail party to welcome a visiting director of the bank. In the past, only supervisors were invited, but my thinking was that there were not many staff at the branch and the added cost would there-fore not be significant. Also, I needed the staff present to help introduce me to customers in attendance with whom they interacted every day. In turn, that act com-municated a certain impression to customers, many of whom commented on it at the cocktail party and during the weeks that followed. So, people on the outside, too, were starting to notice a difference!

We built more momentum by getting involved in community events. This island was known for its boat-racing tradition in which wooden canoes and schooners sailed the surrounding waters, challenging one another for bragging rights in fierce but friendly competition. The corporate community was always a part of this cultural activity—though my bank had never been. This, then, was an opportunity to expose the brand further, and we sponsored one of the boats by paying for a large sail and T-shirts for the crew and supporters, including our staff. Many people singled us out for praise for finally getting involved in this important aspect of the island's culture. While I felt vindicated by seeing the impact on the community at large, I was even more pleased at the pride the staff exhibited at being part of a company that supported such an event.

This positive energy was then channeled into sales activities by staff who were now believers and to a community that had noticed the change and was now receptive to our brand. Staff members were firmly in the boat, believing in the journey and starting to paddle toward our destination. We did more community outreach, and because of customer visits at which staff were more buoyant, the quality of the in-branch customer experience soared.

We ran into some turbulent waters because of inexperience among the staff, but with the assistance of the head office and after bringing in some experienced staff members from the region, the blend of youth and experience made for good team dynamics. By the second year of my tenure in Anguilla, we led the regional country branches, having the highest percentage of loan sales results against target.

Though I was transferred via promotion after my third year in Anguilla, and despite the fact that since that time I have had the opportunity to lead many teams around the region in different areas of banking, I can honestly say that my first two years as manager in Anguilla were my most rewarding assignment. Not only was it my first managerial appointment, it was also important because my conviction in my beliefs and my leadership were vindicated.

As a leader, your role is to open doors, build bridges, and remove barriers. You must teach and coach; you must be firm but fair; you must create the team and make that team the center and the focus. In the end, leadership is about getting employees into the boat and giving them what they need to start paddling.

Principle Five

PROBLEM SOLVING, COURSE CORRECTION

Every day I'm in the office, employees come in to talk to me. My door is always open, and I welcome their visits. Naturally, they are not dropping by to chat; they know I am busy. They have a chain of command and use it. Still, on occasion, some issue arises, and they need to speak to me. In doing so, they are verifying that I am part of their team. They instinctively understand that everything they do affects me, and vice versa.

But that's not how things started out. We may have been in the same boat and headed in the same direction, but not everyone was paddling the same way. Even after our first big meeting and after the smaller one-on-one sessions with each employee, I could see that they were still divided into cliques or had adopted a "we-they" attitude. The mood throughout the agency was corrosive. Many were selfish, having a "me-first" mentality. Others disliked me because I was in the director's office and their former leader wasn't.

That last part was understandable. Some of my new staff members were naturally wary of change, as most people are. Others were concerned that I would not keep my promise to maintain jobs. They felt that the agency's troubles could cause it to fold, taking their positions with it. Others were sure that nothing would be different and rejected anything I said. Only a few people at first were willing to give me a chance.

My challenge, now that I was the chief executive officer, was to change that attitude and create a team. It's the same daunting task that faces any new leader. I was unknown to them; there was no reason for them to embrace me immediately. Their hesitancy was compounded by the reality that I headed a $10-million-a-year agency with dozens of employees. I was responsible not just to them but also to the hundreds of disabled clients who counted on EDCSPIN for services.

Develop Change Agents

Change came slowly. The truth is that old cultures tend to cling with all the tenacity of Velcro. They refuse to disappear. People develop habits based on an existing culture and then conform their activities to it. I was bringing in entirely new concepts: an openness that the staff immediately distrusted because it was so counter to the approach of the previous administration; an emphasis on honesty, which was necessary after problems with the former director; and fairness in hiring and in recognition. That was a lot for anyone to absorb.

All of my subliminal messages and email to employees described earlier could not weld them into a team. I had to start by recognizing the basic reality that my employees came to the agency first to get a job and second because they enjoy helping people. Everything else about them was different, from appearance and background to outside activities and family. They represented varied interests, different ideas. Some would never take the initiative; others would, even if it meant overriding a basic rule. Most, like the majority of employees everywhere, went along with the flow to avoid problems.

My first step was to encourage everyone to focus on the same goal. That divorced the staff from concentrating on personnel changes and policy differences to think about what we all had in common. We were all working hard to provide services to "individuals with developmental disabilities and/or mental retardation" to give them "the opportunity to learn skills needed to reach their highest level of independence all while insuring they experience the same privileges and opportunities enjoyed by all members of our society," as our website states.

That approach then fueled my conversations with my colleagues. I asked each person who met with me the same basic questions: What can we do better? What suggestions can you recommend? How can we resolve problems? That opened the door to constructive criticism and meaningful feedback. Not everyone was willing to speak up, but a handful were willing to trust me and described the working conditions they wanted improved. Several had excellent ideas for implementing the necessary kinds of changes. I wrote them down and, one by one, implemented those that would work. I also credited the employee who proposed the given change.

That was an essential step in the welding process. Many employees simply felt that their voices were not being heard. Previously, they saw how cronies were rewarded while those actually doing the work were shunted aside. Now they saw how I was trying to change the culture within the agency. They were eager to join me. They became my first change agents.

As one person and then the next began to alter attitudes, others followed. I could almost feel the atmosphere lighten. When I first came into the building, employees would glance at me with sullen looks, as if expecting me to morph into some kind of sinister taskmaster. Often, work simply stopped. Staffers waited for me to disappear into my office, as if they had been caught doing something wrong. It was eerie and disheartening to see how employees reacted to my presence.

Eventually, when their fears and negative expectations were clearly not being justified and they saw how various directives evened out workloads and rewarded competency, they began to smile. I could walk in without causing a stir. A couple of people even began to wave or say hello rather than ignoring me. We were becoming a team.

Be Consistent

To maintain the progress, I also realized that the message had to be consistent. It would not help to say one thing and do another. For example, I recall when Ford Motor Company began to advertise in the early 1980s that "Quality is Job 1." The campaign came in response to inroads made by the Japanese automakers into the American automobile market. Unfortunately, Ford merely made claims; the actual manufacture of cars did not catch up to the verbiage. So, buyers began to associate Ford with poorly made cars. That has changed only recently, when the company hype finally began to be matched by quality cars. Today, Ford consistently scores well in quality rankings.

I did not want to be in the position of talking the talk but not walking the walk. As a result, I did not just talk about providing service to clients; I became certified as a professional in compliance and ethics and in health-care compliance. In addition, I became affiliated with numerous professional associations, which allowed me to lecture and conduct research on a variety of topics important to organizations that provide policy, leadership, and development support as well as community, day, and residential services for the disadvantaged. In addition, I became a Cuba Research Delegate with the American Association on Intellectual and Developmental Disabilities.

In 2012, I joined the Harvard Kennedy School Driving Government Performance Consortium. I didn't stop there. I began to write articles on a wide range of topics that were published in *Mental Health News*, *City Limits*, and *USA Today*, and on UrbanTimes.com. Copies of my articles were posted in the office. I saw employees read them, obviously happy that their agency and its director were gaining such attention. People want to be proud of where they work, and positive attention boosts that pride.

In addition, I became active in One Hundred Black Men, Inc., of New York City and a volunteer with PENCIL, Inc., which inspires innovation and improves student achievement by partnering business leaders with public schools. My staff saw that I didn't just talk about community service; I did it.

I firmly believe that any leader must set a standard that everyone else can follow. In addition, for a message to work, it must be repeated. Too often, rumors and innuendo have a way of tunneling into any organization and slowly undermining the best intentions. Therefore, it remains important to make sure that the EDCSPIN vision, which is to Enhance the Quality of Life for People with Disabilities, is clearly represented in the values of the organization. To avoid miscommunication, all the material about EDCSPIN (starting with our vision statement) promotes the same concept: Namely, we provide the best service to our one thousand disabled clients, with an emphasis on five key values:

- Integrity
- Respect
- Opportunity
- Accountability
- Togetherness

Each of these points is continually stressed on our website, in our media releases, and in employee evaluations. They have become an integral aspect of the agency, the lofty goals that each employee tries to ascribe to.

The website further reflects this message with its images of smiling clients and easily accessible information about our mission and values. At the same time, the site includes updates on research in related areas. The pages are bathed in pastel colors that provide warmth and a sense of peace—values that we consistently promote in our day-to-day operations.

The Office: Non-Televised Working Conditions

Aesthetic changes are only a small part of the effort to engage a team in paddling forward together. Employees have to enjoy coming to work, and they have to feel that they are part of an important effort. As a result, I have tried to make EDCSPIN a pleasant place to work, people-wise. And what's good for employees is also good for our clients. No one wants a grumpy social worker showing up at his or her front door or to be greeted by a moody receptionist.

The transformation process involved several steps. First, I eliminated unqualified and underperforming employees who had become far too complacent under the previous administration. I made sure qualified people filled important posts. Staffers were encouraged to continue their education and were then promoted based on their training and abilities, not on their personality or some other arbitrary reason.

Next, knowing that no one is happy working for a supervisor who is inconsiderate or incompetent or incapable, I carefully screened people in leadership roles. Some needed extra training; others—because steps in a process were eliminated or job functions were consolidated or even constant supervision sessions were discontinued—were simply glad to be rid of prior restraints and could function without me constantly looking over their shoulders.

I spent time in my private meetings with employees to identify the quality leaders within the organization. While staffers were often reluctant to discuss the agency as a whole, they didn't hesitate to lambaste department directors and other supervisors they felt were not doing their jobs. That led to more discussions, group meetings, and training sessions.

In most cases, the problems were resolved. A few individuals with titles were invited to prepare their resumes to determine their qualifications and experience. I refused to keep anyone on staff at EDCSPIN who channeled the attitudes or behaviors of the unforgiving, dictatorial boss I'd served under as a lobbyist in Albany.

That meant finding replacements. I told you about my Assistant Executive Director of Programs in an earlier chapter, and I was also able to hire several more very competent replacements. I identified others who may not have wanted a title and the responsibility that goes with it, but who exerted leadership through their actions. Many actual leaders do not have a prominent position. They may be quiet, letting their actions speak for them. They may express opinions, but softly. Mostly, though, they guide consensus simply by their presence. I needed them to buy in.

They did, because they could see I was serious. I really listened to them and then fulfilled promises. Nothing is worse than nodding at some suggestion with the hidden intention of ignoring the idea. If an employee recommended a way to improve some procedure, I looked at it very seriously. I did not simply leap in, of course. Everything has to be tested to locate unseen ramifications. Even when an idea was not adopted, employees could see that I had not lightly dismissed it. I also kept notes so I could explain to the person who had proposed the idea why it had not been implemented.

Fortunately, employees were thrilled that I was even paying attention. They had been ignored for too long. The contrast was between top-down management and the reverse. Too often the American approach has been to let upper management make all the decisions. That does not always work. I'm not suggesting abdicating authority. Rather, I prefer to ensure that everyone affected by any decision has some input into it.

On the other hand, I don't follow the approach pioneered by the Japanese, who hold councils regularly among workers to send proposals to management. Nor do I subscribe to the "management knows best" theory that has dominated American business concepts. My approach is a mix. I am responsible for the final decision, but I seek advice from my staff and welcome their suggestions.

The end result has been an agency that runs efficiently with employees empowered to present ideas, knowing that any appropriate suggestion will be taken seriously. I freely admit that I don't have all the good ideas and greatly appreciate it when staff members provide valuable input. Indeed, we have obtained several grants because of employee suggestions and have also been able to streamline some of our activities.

Situational Management Style

When I first started working in one of the many part-time jobs that helped me pay for college, I really didn't have a management style. I doubt anyone does in that situation.

After all, few of us start at the top of the management chart. I guess if my father had been the head of a company, I might have begun my career with a title, but he worked for the NYC Department of Sanitation. An honorable job (one that afforded me opportunities), but it's not a job with much emphasis on upward mobility.

As a result, I did what most people do: I learned by watching. I had some management background simply from shepherding my siblings about. At the same time, I saw in my immediate family how my grandmother, as matriarch of our extended family, provided leadership, as did my mother. I didn't think of their actions as a management style—the concept was still being born in my mind—but that's what it was. They commanded with their presence, their awareness of everything that was happening in the home and outside, and their concern for the welfare of their f amily members.

From there, I became aware of professors who could guide a classroom rather than dictate to it. I moved on to watching the district attorney and how he kept multiple high-energy and focused professionals—all with diverse agendas and multiple cases—functioning smoothly. Other leaders offered clear images of what not to do. In many ways, that's also very important; role models don't always have to be positive.

For example, I consciously chose to avoid certain lifestyle choices, such as drugs, by observing how people behaved on the street near our apartment. They were slovenly and callous.

They smoked, drank, used drugs, and generally hung around idly. I refused to live like that. I deliberately dressed as well as I could, worked on building a good vocabulary, and established career goals. I was determined not to end up living an unproductive life. Equally, I was an example for my brothers and sisters. As a result, they now own their own businesses or are doing well as employees in various lines of work.

When we were kids at home, I could be direct and almost dictatorial. That style would not work at EDCSPIN, however, where I was trying to build consensus. Managers have to be concerned more about their staff and the organization than their own needs. That requires them to be flexible to match the requirements of the job.

That's why some coaches are successful, while others are not. A young team that needs discipline will not respond to a laissez-faire manager, though a veteran team may. Many times, a leader must shift from one style to another for best results.

Leadership Styles

In his seminal book *Primal Leadership*, internationally known psychologist and former *New York Times* science reporter Daniel Goleman identified six different styles of leadership:

1. Visionary: explaining and guiding in a new direction;
2. Coaching: helping employees improve by connecting goals to performance;

3. Affiliative: building teamwork;

4. Democratic: encouraging staff input;

5. Pacesetting: setting standards; and

6. Commanding: controlling and dictating.

These styles all have strengths and limitations. For example, the visionary style works best when the organization is changing, but it can limit action. It can also cause problems if the new path isn't clearly understood by everyone. Coaching can really help employees, unless they feel they are being micromanaged or don't believe the coach is qualified. The affiliative method reduces conflicts and provides motivation; however, staff have to believe in the leader. If EDCSPIN employees did not accept me, they would not follow my plan.

The democratic concept allows input, but it both slows decision making when action is needed and fails completely when close supervision is required. Our agency was not ready for democracy when I took over, so I waited to implement it. Pacesetting works well with highly motivated staffers who don't need tremendous oversight. However, it can doom morale by causing employees who fail to reach the high bar to feel like failures. It also causes problems when teams are working on projects, because someone in the group may fall short.

Commanding remains popular but really works only

when immediate decisions are needed. Otherwise, it can undercut job satisfaction, particularly when the "commander" is a despot.

Success requires finding the right fit at the right time. In my case, when I was called into the agency, action was needed to right the boat and to reassure the employees. I could not wait for input or simply dictate. Instead, I articulated the vision of the agency and encouraged team building. From there, I moved into the democratic approach, seeking ideas from my staff.

I believe any leader must be flexible that way. Success comes by recognizing when one approach isn't working and another should be tried. Furthermore, each style has these three internal elements: Directing, Discussing, and Delegating.

Directing

The directing element of management has to be professional, concise, and direct. Employees must know what's happening. Failure to communicate invites rumors, which can quickly erode any progress.

A leader cannot abdicate his or her role. I couldn't let someone else conduct the first meeting; the staff would have figured that I was only a figurehead. Any information to the staff in the form of email and directives also had to carry my name. I had to direct. Then my job was to tell an employee what to do and how to do it. Communication was one-way: from me to the staff. It had to be precise and provide an overview of my thinking. That established my credibility to lead the agency. As I mentioned earlier, employees need the important details, but they don't need to be bogged down with excessive facts that can confuse the situation. This approach worked very well when I first arrived but was quickly abandoned so that skilled staffers did not feel micromanaged.

Discussing

The discussion element of management followed. In the private meetings and later in large-group sessions, I invited employees to provide their input; I became a facilitator. This works by asking questions, such as: "What could have been done better?" "Do you have suggestions for how you can improve?" and so on. Here, I didn't want to dictate, but to encourage employees to find their path to improvements.

In group meetings, I knew what I wanted the staff to decide on a particular course of action and, through questions and suggestions, helped guide the decision. In other situations, employees came up with results that differed from what I thought was best but that turned out to be a great choice.

In all cases, discussions cannot be dominated by a few individuals—including the CEO. This has to be a democratic process where everyone feels free to provide input and is given the opportunity to do so. "What do you think?" is a great opener for any discussion.

Delegating

Finally, I learned to delegate and then let the designated employee do her job. This third internal element created empowerment. Employees then develop as individuals: improving, learning, and feeling more in control of their own careers. Most people learn best by doing. They cannot function, however, with someone breathing down their necks; they are afraid to be creative or to risk making a mistake.

Managers must make sure that each and every employee knows exactly what to do. Nebulous instructions can hamstring anyone. At the same time, dates need to be assigned for each deliverable. I set the schedule in accordance with the employee's expectations: When does he think he can finish a particular portion of the assigned task? Such deadlines need to be realistic but enforced.

Delegation leads to recognition. Someone who took on a task—such as organizing a special event or arranging for visitors to tour the agency—and handled it well deserves to be praised publicly. Private commendations are nice, but employees typically prefer that their peers know about their accomplishments. Donations may be given anonymously, but praise deserves an audience.

Employee Input Required

As you can tell, employee participation is the key to successful implementation of any style of leadership. Obviously, if staff members decline to get involved, any idea, no matter how good, will deflate quickly. That's also true if employees feel they cannot contribute.

In some management styles, such as the one I endured in Albany, no one is supposed to say anything; just listen and obey. But all that did was stifle creativity.

This problem is nationwide, by the way. A 2012 survey by Fierce, Inc., a communication training and leadership organization, found that many employees "believe many workplace practices aren't effective and often get in the way of performance results."[1] At the same time, nearly 50 percent of employees thought that management failure to explain how decisions are made and the lack of employee input hurt productivity. The solution is to ask employees to offer their ideas.

In the past, companies used to put out suggestion boxes. Then, on some undefined day, some boss wearily sat down and read the occasional entry. Often, the box was a repository for insults or isolated complaints. A few suggestions might even be anatomically impossible. The box also really didn't encourage participation, since everyone could see who was submitting the suggestion. Many employees resorted to early morning forays or other surreptitious methods of dropping a note in the box.

These days, the box seems so old-fashioned. With computers, any employee can quietly submit an idea or a comment without a colleague knowing about it. However, this approach is not completely anonymous, since the person reading the email knows where it came from.

An alternative is a survey. In this approach, the person reading the results has no idea who submitted them. This method is used at universities, where students can evaluate their instructors without fearing any repercussions. The survey is done online but does not record who filled it out.

Survey questions have to be carefully written if the results are to be useful. Questions that are too general won't provide the necessary feedback to help a manager address a situation. The type of questions also has to vary, perhaps including some with a five-point scale from very satisfactory to unsatisfactory and others that are open ended and require written feedback.

The survey can't be too long. Our clients need attention, and every minute that a staffer does something else detracts from services. Experts suggest that thirty-five to fifty-five questions are sufficient. Regardless, any survey shouldn't take more than twenty-five minutes to complete. More than that, and the process seems like an imposition.

A good survey should garner up to 90 percent participation.

I use staff meetings before work to hand out surveys and let employees fill them out. Some employees who miss the meeting can fill the survey out later and place it in a receptacle so I don't know who answered the questions.

Surveys are not the only option. These days, any organization can set up an online site where employees can leave messages and suggestions. They can identify themselves or remain anonymous. Then, too, there's always the suggestion box; modern technology hasn't replaced it entirely yet.

Any request for information or ideas creates an implied commitment from management to follow up. My employees need to know their voices are heard. Josh Greenberg, president of AlphaMeasure, a research firm based in Boulder, Colorado, noted that "If you're going to collect all this data and then not close the loop back to the employees it almost makes sense not to do the survey. It's important to let them know that they've been heard."[2]

I use meetings to introduce changes or new plans based on the surveys and suggestions I've received. By making public announcements at group meetings, agency employees know that I care about their input from surveys or suggestions. Nothing falls flatter than a survey without the backing of management.

Once employees see that a leader is serious about making improvements and that positive changes are being made, they begin to feel empowered. They begin to coalesce into a team.

Briefly stated, here are the steps I followed to achieve that goal:

- ◇ Create a vision.
- ◇ Define everyone's role within that vision.
- ◇ Set long-term and short-term goals.
- ◇ Clearly communicate the vision and goals.
- ◇ Set a schedule and stick to it.
- ◇ Ask for input and accept criticism and advice.
- ◇ Don't expect immediate results; change takes time.
- ◇ Recognize employees who achieve set goals.
- ◇ Always encourage.
- ◇ Be flexible.
- ◇ Delegate.

It worked at my agency. Within a year after taking over at EDCSPIN, I could see that attitudes had shifted. That reality is clearly visible on the bottom line: Today, EDCSPIN has a $25 million annual budget and more than five hundred employees. Every one of them is doing a great job.

As steel magnate Andrew Carnegie said: "Teamwork is the ability to work together toward a common vision; the ability to direct individual accomplishments toward organizational objectives. It is the fuel that allows common people to attain uncommon results."[3]

I really believe it was the turning point of my life when I

took this large group of people, many of whom resented me because I replaced their beloved director and none of whom had a real bond with one another, and turned them into a meaningful team that is paddling together and enthusiastically working for the community.

◆ ◆ ◆

Alfredo Giovine's "Perspective" essay explains the traditional Italian background he came from and built on. He discusses his core values, the qualities he looks for in his staff, and how he was able to develop his restaurant business and make it an integral part of the community in Barbados.

PERSPECTIVE: TAPAS WITH A VIEW

Alfredo Giovine

I was born in the south of Italy, in Bari. In Italy, you finish your secondary school at eighteen and then you go to university. Fortunately, I had the opportunity to get admitted into a very popular academy in Milan.

When I moved to Milan, I started to live on my own. That, of course, was a big difference because you start to be responsible for your own life. You can eat when you want; you can sleep when you want; you do your foolishness and partying; but again you are responsible. I took university very seriously, but I saw friends go back home after the first year because life in another city by yourself can be rather challenging.

I graduated with a degree in economics. I never had any experience with restaurants or the food business because it was never my first interest. I ended up living in Colombia for almost two years by chance, because I got a job distributing Italian food and products. That was my first contact with the food business. When I came to Barbados, it was because I was partnering with other people who were opening an Italian restaurant, and that became the first commercial experience I had in the food business.

I cannot say restaurants were my life. I ended up in the restaurant business because I liked the relationships with the people. I also like it because it is labor intensive. You open every day for many hours per day—it's not nine to five—and then you go home. And even when I go home, I still have to check what's going on with the business.

Of course, because it's mine I want to make sure everything goes well, but I also really like to be sure all my customers are happy. For example, if I make a special pasta just for you that is not on the menu, you feel very honored and happy. For me, it's nothing major: I have the kitchen; I have the products in the fridge. Just give me the time to cook it, and I will make you happy. The different perspective is amazing. For me, it's my daily job. For you, it's like "Wow, Alfredo made pasta dishes just for me."

So, you can really and truly make people happy without a big effort; that's my bottom line. I always tell the guys, "I want whoever leaves this establishment to leave happy." I want my employees to embrace that goal and work together to achieve it.

When I hire staff—waiters, hosts, bartenders—I look to see if you are naturally nice. If you are, you can learn how to do this job. Serving people is not hard: You learn how to pour the wine; you learn where to put the cups. But to really be nice, to smile at people, to be pleasant— you cannot train or create that; it has to be inside. I have to find people who like to share most of their time with other people. You have to be committed to the goal of customer satisfaction, and you have to care about their dining experience.

Having the opportunity to travel has always been something that I liked. And for me, travel means going somewhere, meeting the people of that place, spending my time with them, and sharing as much as I can of my experience and their experience. I brought new things to Barbados, but Barbados also had a lot of things that were new to me. It's a reciprocal sharing of experience.

For example, when people asked me about Italian wine or food, I realized that even though I never studied it, I knew a lot because I lived it, watching TV, hearing my parents talk. So, I have a lot of knowledge about wine and food, not because I was reading it in books or studying it but simply because I experienced it in my environment.

I have lived in a number of places—South America, Venezuela, Costa Rica, and Italy—and I have traveled a lot through Europe and the United States. I have already spent ten years in Barbados, and I can say that I have decided to live out my life here.

The culture in Barbados is a very level playing field: businessmen sharing their experience with ordinary people or paying their own bills in the supermarket line. The other day, a government minister was standing in line in front of me at the supermarket. In Italy, privilege is everywhere—because I am so-and-so, I don't go to the supermarket and buy my own cigarettes. But here, at the end of the day, people live their lives as they see fit. So, I find the society here very fair and very honest.

I grew up in a family where everyone had plenty of freedom to think about the future without the pressure of expectations. For example, my dad graduated in pharmacology but ended up being a writer and opened his own publishing house. I come from a background where people are doing what they really feel they need to do; I've never been stuck in a specific career track.

I came to Barbados because I received a call that there was an Italian couple the same age as my mom and dad who were opening a delicatessen, and they were looking for somebody to help them run this place. I had met them when I was distributing food products and living in Colombia. They asked if I was interested, and at the time, I was just finishing my internship in Colombia. I decided I'd go to Barbados for a few months to help these people open their business.

I had to learn to deal with customers on a day-to-day basis, and that's when I realized I really liked it. The couple who were my business partners helped me a lot. First of all, because they were my parents' age, they took me in and treated me like their son, for which I was really grateful. They were very kind, and I learned a lot from them, and of course, I gave them all my energy and passion.

Mama Mia was a typical Italian deli, offering pasta, pizza, and sandwiches, with all the ingredients brought in from Italy. The deli was very successful because it was something new for Barbados at a time when Bajans (Barbadians) started to open up to different types of food. Bajans have started to travel more and experience different foods. That was one of the key elements that made Mama Mia a success.

I ran Mama Mia for six years for the couple. Then, in 2009, two other Italian guys who were living here and I took over and reopened as Tapas. We refreshed the place, which has a very nice spot right in front of the ocean, and we made a good deal with the previous management and landlord. After six months, one of the three who was less involved realized it made no sense to stay, so we bought him out. Now it is just two of us: the chef and me. One runs the kitchen; the other runs the floor. We share all the duties and responsibilities equally, so each one does his part. The great thing is that each of us has a very high respect for the other. I don't step into the kitchen and say, "I know this should have more salt or be served with this sauce." I simply pass on my advice or suggestions and what I hear on the floor: "Yes, people like it," or "No, they don't like it." But if I have a problem with the kitchen staff, though I am an owner of the business, I don't go and deal with the kitchen staff. I tell my partner, Franco, "John had this problem yesterday," or "I had this problem with John. You sort it out. It's your guy." This way, we maintain the reputation and respect that the two of us have with the relative staff.

Whatever happens on the floor is my responsibility; whatever happens in the kitchen is his. This has been a key point for me. You manage your duties and responsibilities, and you know that you are the only chief in your area. I think that in this kind of environment you need to have a very clear chain of command because, at the end of the day, it is the kind of business where problems have to be solved extremely quickly. For example, if a customer complains about a dish, I don't have the time to say, "Come tomorrow and I will give you some different food." The customer is looking for a solution now. So, for me, it is very important that the roles and responsibilities are clear to everybody so that everyone knows where to go and how to operate.

We have sixty people employed at Tapas, and our common goal is to provide a great customer experience. To achieve that goal, we must be clear when giving direction and assigning tasks. Managing sixty people in a fixed space requires excellent choreography, so it is especially important that each person moves in the same direction, toward the same goal. At Tapas, we try to do this in ways that reflect the proud culture of Barbados.

For example, people here are very honest and hospitable. Barbados is the kind of place where if your wallet falls out of your pocket 95 percent of people will pick it up to give it back to you exactly as you lost it. One of the other things that also impress tourists is that if you stop on the road and ask for directions, many times people will say, "Follow me." It's a very friendly place. So, of course, we want our restaurant to reflect that as well.

To give you an idea, one night just after we first opened Tapas, during closing I forgot to shut the main door. Because we went out the back door, the main door was left open, and I didn't realize it. At 2:00 a.m., a policeman came to my house—it's a small island, so the policeman knew where I lived—and said, "Alfredo, there is a problem at Tapas. Come with me."

When I got there, I realized the door was open. I had left the restaurant at around 11:00 p.m., and for three or four hours anyone could have helped themselves to all the liquor and spirits, but no one took anything. Someone called the police and said, "Look, Tapas is open, and no one is there." There are many more stories like this.

Right in front of the restaurant there is a boardwalk that the city built a few years ago. That has become a very nice location, because it is the only place on the island that you can really walk along the ocean without cars passing. Coming from a city in the south of Italy, I enjoy regular strolls along the ocean, just meeting friends and having a beer on the plaza—a meeting place like residents enjoyed in Roman and Greek times. That is what I imagined would happen with this boardwalk, and that is what it has become now.

I have a slice of Barbados passing in front of me every day. It not only helps my business, but it also helps my relationships with people. One day you have a little one who wants a glass of water, and another day someone has a small accident and needs rubbing alcohol for his knee. They are small things, but they foster the sense of family, of community, where everyone is there for one another.

This kind of togetherness, where everyone helps one another, is important to Barbadians. We understand that we are all in this thing called life together, and we'll all prosper if we work together toward a common goal.

Principle Six

EVERY CREW MEMBER MATTERS

~~~

My individual interviews with EDCSPIN employees went well, for the most part. I understood they would be nervous, but I expected them to treat me with respect. Only a couple of people were what I considered rude. One young man, for example, sauntered in, draped himself over the chair, and paid little attention to anything I said.

Over time, I have learned that his behavior, while inappropriate, was not unique. In every company or organization, there are invariably a few people who don't seem to fit in or even want to. They usually don't last long, but I encourage leaders to tolerate that kind of behavior from individuals who are also making valuable contributions. (I don't advocate total insubordination or rudeness, of course, no matter how productive the individual.) Otherwise, we risk draining the creativity that often comes with slightly unusual behavior. For example, with someone who's very productive, you might overlook the occasional late arrival to work, unconventional clothing or hairstyle, the tendency to chat a bit too long with coworkers, and the like. But not to the point of allowing them to flout the rules or of showing favoritism that others could complain about.

Address Difficult People

Here are some of the difficult staffers I've had to deal with and the course I chose in handling each person's challenges:

Egotists. These folks think they are special. So, they tend to shun time clocks and take breaks whenever the urge appears. Their work is often excellent, though, and as a result, I want them to stay. But I don't want the headaches they cause. Their behavior can lead to two problems: First, their demands can get excessive, overshadowing value. Second, other employees may chafe when they see someone getting special benefits. I try to treat everyone the same, but demands of certain jobs require them to be there when the front door opens. In one particular case, I had to reprimand a perpetually late prima donna, which undermined his enthusiasm. I didn't want him to quit, so finally we discussed ways to resolve the concern. I then put him in a position where flexible hours were part of the job. (This highlights the difference between having hourly workers and salaried ones. Salaried workers might work sixty hours a week yet be paid for only forty, but they might be allowed some flexibility in their work schedule where permitted. Hourly workers usually do not have flexible schedules.) He has been very good since then.

Not doing anything would not have helped. Inactivity creates a vicious circle, with resentment rising as the prima donna follows her or his own rules. That in turn undermines trust between management and staff. Trust is a key component in any organization's success, so as a result, most of us would be better off without such individuals. Stars may drive the worlds of sports and entertainment, but once they enter the working world, they need to fit in for the benefit of everyone. If my prima donna hadn't adjusted and accepted the new job, I would have reluctantly asked him to leave.

Nitpickers. Some people want everything to be perfect. That's helpful as long as it doesn't interfere with production. But when someone quibbles over every aspect of a project, there can be problems, as well as a real dilemma. We each want whatever we do to represent our best work; consequently, we want to correct any mistakes. At the same time, however, we face deadlines for grant submissions and other projects. We had a nit-picking perfectionist at the agency who was causing havoc with our ability to submit applications and other documents on time. My first choice was to discuss the deadlines with everyone and to be sure there was ample time to meet them. I also assigned the perfectionist to help with the planning, but kept her away from the final process. Of course, we could have made sure every project was completed perfectly, but that's improbable. We simply do the best we can. We focus on finding and correcting major errors, not every mistake.

Innovators. These people are always thinking ahead but get distracted from the job at hand. For example, I have an employee who is extraordinarily creative. She has found ways of streamlining several processes, and I don't want to discourage her. After all, ideas are the lifeblood of any organization. On the other hand, today's work has to be done. She wasn't completing anything because she was so busy coming up with new ways to do something. That, in turn, antagonized her colleagues, who were forced to do her work as well as their own. My answer was to create an outlet for her to submit ideas. We would talk about them, and at the same time, I carefully monitored her assigned tasks, making sure they were completed as required and on time. She got the hint soon enough, and I have ended up with a valuable employee.

Create a Process

In each situation I just described, I followed a clear process that was obvious to the staff. It told everyone that creativity would be rewarded but that anything that damaged the agency or created turmoil among employees would not be acceptable. The steps in the process provided tactics for dealing with problem employees, allowing me to isolate the concern and reduce the chances that the employee's negative traits and behaviors would infect the rest of the agency.

Communicate. This mutes the grousing, prunes back the grapevine, and shuts down the rumor mill. I always keep my door open and immediately let employees know what is happening that affects them. Material is posted on the website, sent in email to employees, and, if necessary, posted in writing. There's no reason for any employee not to know the truth. This was vitally important when I became the director; I had to stifle claims that people would be fired or jobs would be eliminated. It also strengthened my position when none of the negative rumors proved to be true and the communication from my office was accurate.

Be active. I can't just sit in my office. I walk around; I talk to employees. They know I'm the leader and may not be in a position to be completely open about everything that's going on in the background; however, the more they see me and realize that we're working together, the more they are willing to tell me their concerns. I want them to raise any concerns to me, not simply spout objections into the office where they can infect others.

Outline the procedure. The staff need to know that inappropriate negative comments or the spreading of false reports has consequences. I don't expect everything to be rosy all the time, but I do expect concerns to be channeled through the right process so they can be addressed. Employees who fail to follow the channels can expect reprimands based on a clearly stated procedure.

Get good employees. That's really the best choice. Hire people with positive attitudes; that is, the kind who don't carp but look for solutions. Following this broad approach, I have greatly reduced negativity at the agency, enabling us to focus on helping our clients. Unfortunately, I haven't reached everyone; no one can. There are always some employees who test limits, violate basic rules, and generally cause havoc through actions, words, or both. Dealing with them has required a very different process.

I certainly do not get involved in personnel matters unless the situation is significant. I don't want to hold a formal, in-office meeting with someone who is upset over something minor. A brief conversation in the hallway suffices.

For the more significant breaches, I have to be sure the employees were really exhibiting bad behavior. After all, something I think is unacceptable may seem perfectly normal to someone else. It's easy to misunderstand. I can't even count the number of times I misconstrued something only because I heard part of a conversation or saw some gesture out of context. I am sure everyone else has had similar experiences.

Besides, people have different upbringings and culture. Sometimes, I just have to whisper a comment to someone to eliminate the problem. I don't want to embarrass the person, but I want the particular action stopped.

Determine Guidelines: Results Matter

Sometimes, a simple example takes care of the problem. Everyone needs guidelines. The easiest solution is simply letting someone know how I want the phone answered or the best way to deal with an overbearing parent. I do not accept any finger-pointing or excuses. The cause of a problem does not matter; staff will simply need to work out a solution that ends the disruptions. The agency's expectations must be respected. If I have a choice, I will always opt for the simplest option, the one with the fewest disruptions in the agency's life and the one that preserves the employee's job.

For example, two squabbling employees can create turmoil in an office. Because of their jobs, they regularly interact, but their bickering is cutting into productivity and annoying their colleagues. My approach is to speak directly to both of them, letting them know that their petty difference cannot be allowed to undermine their work. I expect them to be responsible and professional while on the job. Of course, they will be told that further disruptions could have serious consequences.

The point is to address the situation quickly and firmly. Any misbehaving employees need to understand what is expected of them while working for the agency. They may need some coaching to learn new strategies. For instance, new employees may never have worked in an agency or had to function on teams before. My role then is to encourage the employees while carefully monitoring progress. People are held accountable for their actions, but they must know which actions are inappropriate and must be changed.

This can be a lengthy process, but any employee deserves the opportunity unless the behavior is particularly egregious, such as stealing or physically attacking someone else. I create a timetable with milestones the employee is expected to reach en route to a change in behavior. That may include counseling sessions, training, or just a commitment to learn office procedures.

The employee may be asked to apologize to the offended parties, just to help rebuild trust and camaraderie. That's a hard step for anyone but also an indication of a willingness to improve.

Of course, I can't be naïve. Some people will say all the right things and do the opposite. Nevertheless, with the proper approach, I have been able to retain good employees and eliminate inappropriate behavior.

Typically, the infighting and loud arguments are rare and can be handled swiftly. Unfortunately, not everything is that smooth, especially when a serious breach of agency rules occurs. In such a circumstance, everyone is watching to see what happens. Will I uphold the rules, especially if an important worker is involved? The answer is important. Other employees usually don't like to endure misbehaving colleagues for very long. They also lose respect when the rules aren't applied equally.

My only choice, then, is to follow a set process that the employees are informed of when hired. It's part of their employment manual and explained in meetings.

They face meetings and official reprimands following violation of known company policy and other major transgressions. For example, an employee who steals from his colleagues creates a dangerous situation for clients. Someone who misrepresents himself, fails to file the necessary reports, makes false claims for insurance purposes, or performs similar misdeeds also falls into that category. Major misbehavior like that requires immediate, decisive intervention.

Documentation is important, both for fairness and for legal concerns. The employees need to know that everyone is treated fairly and equally. Documentation helps show that the correct action was taken and that it was consistent from one staffer to the next. Privacy laws prevent sharing the information, but everyone knows when I ask someone to leave that I have sufficient evidence and cause.

At the same time, as a lawyer, I am well aware that the agency could end up in court if a former employee felt discriminated against or unfairly fired. The documents amassed in an employee file provide a legal basis for any action I take.

Regardless of what I think I should do, I always meet with any employee who has committed a serious transgression. I make sure either the employee's supervisor and/or the head of human resources joins us. That way, the session won't descend into a shouting contest. I rarely get upset, but any person called into a serious, employment-related meeting with a boss can get accusatory.

The usual problems are related to trust. Unfortunately, many people are wary of trusting others. They build walls and lash out inappropriately. They don't want anyone to "intrude" into their workspace or activities. They think the worst: Something will be said or done to hurt them—something will be misconstrued. They want to be appreciated and thanked, but instead, they create an atmosphere that causes the opposite results. So, they get to see me.

Firing really has to be the last step. As we all know, it takes time and money to hire and train a replacement. One lengthy study demonstrated that companies pay 20 percent of a worker's salary to replace her. That includes the loss of productivity while waiting for the replacement to get up to speed.

Considering how often people change jobs in a normal economy, it's always a good idea, then, to retain good workers. I hope this process helps a "problem child" learn the errors of his ways and straighten out.

Elements of the Resolution

Our agency's process, which I just outlined, has some easily discernible elements.

◇ **Be open and honest.** Examples help illustrate the concern. Many times employees are really bewildered about why I am disappointed about something they did. The event didn't register with them. A reminder helps.

◇ **Obtain all points of view.** If the meeting is in regard to a major upheaval, then I want to know what happened from the employee's point of view and from the perspective of everyone involved. This testimony helps create a clear picture in situations where I did not witness the event or have only a written complaint from a client's family to go on.

◇ **Ask what message the employee was sending.** If his plan was to be belligerent, then the path to discuss proper behavior is open. There's a psychological aspect here: We all have self-concepts. We all see ourselves one way and want others to see us that way. Employees see themselves as good people. Any discussion that explains how they allowed themselves to be seen differently can have an impact on future behavior.

⋄ **Explain the impact.** Opportunities for raises and promotions often motivate staff members. Bad behavior can reduce those chances. Highlighting that reality often causes a slacker to rethink what happened and how it can hurt her in the future.

⋄ **Provide alternatives.** An employee who feels frustrated and lashes out may not think of more orderly solutions, such as talking to personnel, a boss, or even me. I prefer that people use the chain of command, but I also understand that sometimes people want to go straight to the top. That's why my office door is always open. The point is to let any employee know there are good choices and bad ones. The hope is to nudge them toward making the good one. That involves providing the information needed to make the correct decision. Many of my employees work alone with clients. Confronted with a strange situation, they may not know what to do and may feel completely helpless. Bad decisions can be made in those situations. With information, the employee knows she is not isolated and that there is help.

⋄ **Be proactive.** I try to be aware of what's happening in the office. I want to try to cut off any problem before it arises. For example, if deadlines are approaching, staffers working on a project may be nervous and concerned. Frayed nerves can lead to confrontations.

A respite at a restaurant, a chance to refresh and regroup, can help resolve a potential blowup before it happens.

◇ **Listen to individual speech.** Sometimes the chronic complainer is speaking only for him- or herself, but there are times when the person might be reflecting the feelings of a whole department. That's why it's never a good idea to totally ignore the complaints. Check with colleagues and coworkers to see if there's any validity to the claims.

◇ **Be patient.** Change takes a while. Sometimes, a schedule is necessary: I may expect a medical report or completion of an anger-management program by a certain date, for example. That gives people room to work while reducing the stress related to uncertainty. After all, we are all works in progress. I always consider several points before taking any action: (1) Is the situation permanent, requiring action? Or will it slowly disappear? Most things just dissipate in time. (2) Does it really matter? Most problems really do not impact the agency or our ability to provide the needed service. As a result, I might be better off giving the air time to clear.

◇ **Be aware of other changes.** Now and again, employees feel threatened and act accordingly when conditions at work change or there's a shift in responsibilities. If the employee has been productive in the past, I will sit down with him and try to determine what the real problem is. Then, together we can come up with a solution.

◇ **Have witnesses.** I have to be careful to avoid the appearance of bias. As a result, I try to include the personnel director or a board member in an evaluation that could end in termination. I turn over all the notes and memos and encourage whoever sat in the meeting to offer an opinion. I still make the final decision, but input helps ensure that I make the appropriate one.

In the end, some employees will change and prove their value while others will have to leave. The young man who sprawled across the chair in our lone meeting, for instance, had to grow up somewhere else. By asking him to leave, I affirmed company values while setting a standard for everyone. The others who stayed after a meeting with me demonstrated that mistakes can be corrected, that everyone can learn, and that I want to do what is best for both the employee and the agency.

Those are valuable lessons that cut to the core of the agency's vision and create a lasting impression. Setting the bar high can be very valuable for ensuring a long-term and successful future.

◆ ◆ ◆

Guy Stanley Philoche, a painter, understands better than most the importance of each disparate element to the creation of a unified whole. In this final "Perspective" essay, he discusses his commitment to his work, touching on truth versus fame in the arts, his search for community, and above all, being true to oneself.

PERSPECTIVE: BEAUTIFUL ORGANIZATION OF CHAOS

Guy Stanley Philoche

When I was a kid, I got lost in comic books and became a huge Disney fan. When everybody else went out to recess, I would get my comic book, read it, and try to copy everything. In my early childhood, I'd wake up and watch Disney cartoons while eating a big bowl of cereal. I wanted to create that world.

I realized I could draw really well when I was in the second or third grade. I drew a picture and the teacher asked me, "Did you trace that?"

I said, "What's tracing?"

She said, "Oh, wow, you can really draw."

But my big "Aha!" moment was probably going to the museums for the first time on a class trip and seeing the masterpieces—Picasso, van Gogh—all those greats. That's when I realized I wanted to be an artist. Ever since then, every time we had to do a report on someone, I always chose an artist. It was always about an artist that I loved.

After high school, once I got to art school, I met other people like myself, people who liked to draw. They weren't athletes or scholars, but I surrounded myself with people who could relate to me. That's one of the keys to success: surrounding yourself with people who are into the same things that you are into and who are all really positive. All that rubs off, and you feed off one another.

I remember my first big New York show. I sent a car to pick up my family in Connecticut. I remember my dad looking at my paintings, looking at the titles of everything, and he started noticing these little red dots next to the paintings. He asked me what the dots meant. I said, "It means they're sold." He was like, "Holy shit, you really are famous."

I said, "Not yet, but I'm working on it." That was probably one of the coolest moments: when my dad actually realized that this is what his son does—he's a painter.

But allow me to be super honest. Being an artist is not glamorous or sexy. I made tons and tons of sacrifices. All my friends are having kids and getting married, and I'm still just painting; I don't see myself doing anything else.

I've sold paintings because someone saw me delivering one on the subway. These are not urban legends; these are true stories that happen to real New Yorkers because your life really could change in a heartbeat. I always believed it was important to just keep your eye on the prize. I didn't come here to find love or to have a kid. I came for one purpose only: to be in the Museum of Modern Art.

One of the concepts of the "Everybody Paddles" movement that caught my attention was the notion of everybody pursuing a common goal. That's what I mean by keeping your eye on the prize. If you don't keep your eyes on your goal, it is easy to lose your way. My paintings are an attempt to bring order out of chaos in my own life. Even though I have pursued a career in which I work alone, I appreciate the importance of people working together as a community.

The community aspect in the art world is different. Working together as a community doesn't exist in the art world these days. It did back in the 1960s and 1970s, when Jackson Pollock and Jasper Johns looked out for each other. People are cutthroat now. I know super-famous artists, and I also know struggling artists.

Famous artists are protective of their collectors' contacts; if they have any sense of competition, they feel you're stealing money from them. But in my case, every time I sell a painting, I tend to buy a painting from someone who is not well known.

People come to my studio and they ask, "Why do you collect art?" I believe in karma; you need to share love and look out for each other. For art to flourish, artists must also flourish, and the best way for that to happen is for artists to work together toward that common goal. Some of my work has been referred to as a "beautiful organization of chaos." I think there is something about the "Everybody Paddles" movement that speaks to that concept. It is a simple thing, but if we could remove the chaos of our everyday lives by simply working together, at the same time, toward a common goal, one can only imagine how beautiful our lives could be. That, to me, would be amazing.

CONCLUSION

It's been an interesting journey to this point. By now you've seen how to overcome separate units inside any organization; how to motivate employees through fair, consistent treatment; how to handle complaints; the value of good, transparent communication; and the importance of mission and vision statements and consequent actions.

Following these guidelines, anyone can be an excellent leader, and a team can be built and maintained. However, there's one more aspect to consider: moving away from self-interest and toward serving others. Good managers do not just direct; they also recognize their role as a facilitator, as a role model, and as an instrument for helping others achieve their success.

Motivational speaker Anthony Robbins put the feeling this way: "Only those who have learned the power of sincere and selfless contribution experience life's deepest joy: True Fulfillment."[1]

The problem for all of us, including me, is that for a long time life was simply about *me*. It had to be; remember the quote from Hillel? "If I am not for myself, who will be?" We have all, at various times, focused on achievement and gaining success. Conversations were built around how much *I* wanted to accomplish my career goals, how stressful the whole process was for *me*, how *I* could better *my* chances, and so forth.

It seemed that the only pronouns I was familiar with were *I* and *me*. The more I focused on where I wanted to go, the less I focused on the true purpose that we have on this earth. As time progressed, however, I became open to the possibility of selfless action, which, paradoxically, can be the most self-fulfilling action; it gave me purpose.

More and more, I realize just how selfish we human beings naturally are. All of us have a tendency to be self-centered, even though many of us may not be willing to admit it. In truth, however, leaders have to be able to put themselves second and others first. That's how people get motivated to do their work. My agency provides services twenty-four hours a day; I also have to be available all the time. I have to respect everyone who is contributing, who is paddling alongside me. I have to be flexible and willing to change in order to benefit someone else.

I need to live a life that is centered on serving others, meeting their needs, and giving of myself to accomplish what is best for them. By doing so, I demonstrate the two key traits that every successful leader must embody:

◇ **Kindness.** I have worked under tyrants; maybe you have too. Kindness accomplishes far more.

◇ **Integrity.** This is revealed when no one is looking at you. A leader with integrity is emulated and admired. The end result is that not only do your employees want you to guide them: They are eager to pick up their paddles and join you.

And now we come to the time to act. I have talked about change, but such words have no meaning without some action behind them. We see that happen throughout society; nothing really happens, even as the rhetoric rolls on. We remain stagnant and cannot move.

The solution is to commit to being a better leader. Think of it as a New Year's resolution you really keep.

◇ Act beyond expectations.
◇ Act along with your words.
◇ Act with your voice, all the time.
◇ Act at work, at home, and throughout your community.
◇ Act when no one else is looking.
◇ Act, even if you are the only one.

Now . . . you are ready to pick up your paddle and start moving forward. Others will follow.

ABOUT THE CONTRIBUTORS

Peter F. Borish currently serves as chairman and CEO of Computer Trading Corporation, an actively managed fund focused on macroeconomic investing. Three decades of experience in the financial futures and derivatives markets have provided Mr. Borish with an in-depth understanding of global markets and their complexities. He brings a valuable perspective as an asset manager, seasoned investor, and corporate adviser to critical financial discussions.

An investor in and a board member of CharityBuzz.com, an innovative company that assists nonprofits, Mr. Borish's career began at the Federal Reserve Bank of New York, where he monitored foreign-exchange futures and options. He is a founding member of the board of directors of the Robin Hood Foundation, which funds New York City educational projects for disadvantaged children, as well as a mayoral appointee to the Youth Board of the New York City Department of Youth and Community Development and a board member of the Math for America Foundation.

Kennedy Swaratsingh specializes in private enterprises, nonprofit organizations, and public service in Trinidad and Tobago. He is currently serving as a consultant to Ernst & Young Caribbean, a global leader in assurance, tax, transactions, and advisory services, working closely with governments throughout the region on development projects and international funding mechanisms. Prior to joining Ernst & Young Caribbean, Mr. Swaratsingh served as director of business solutions for Digicel Group Limited (DGL). He was responsible for the region of Barbados and the OESC Islands, managing a global resource, ethical corporate behavior, social investments, and environmental affairs.

Previously, he served as chief operating officer for the Crane Residential Resorts, president of the Caribbean Telecommunication Union, minister of public administration, and member of Parliament for the Constituency of Saint Joseph.

Mr. Swaratsingh was ordained a Catholic priest in 1991 and serves several parishes in Trinidad.

Theodore Hanley, MD, a board-certified anesthesiologist with over twenty years of experience at leading hospitals across the New York City area, now serves as chair of anesthesiology and pain management at Woodhull Hospital, North Brooklyn Health Network, Health and Hospital Corporation. Additionally, he currently serves as assistant professor of anesthesiology at NYU School of Medicine.

Previously, Dr. Hanley served as chief of anesthesiology at Saint Barnabas Hospital in New York City. Dr. Hanley also founded and served as president and CEO of Madison Pain Management, which provided full anesthesia coverage to two major health-care facilities, including Manhattan Psychiatric Center and North General Hospital, where he also served as president of the medical staff and chair of the executive committee, the credentials committee, and the bylaws committee.

Since 2002, Dr. Hanley has been a proud traveling member of the Doctors on Call surgical outreach team, a private nonprofit committed to providing surgical aid in the Caribbean.

Stacie Henderson joined Westfield World Trade Center as the vice president of marketing after spending over seven years at Versace. In her current role, she oversees brand positioning, advertising, digital, public relations, and tourism for the new retail district that will open at the World Trade Center in March 2015.

Ms. Henderson was the vice president of marketing and events for Versace USA. In this role, she had the responsibility for developing and executing marketing strategies for six brands and multiple product categories for the global fashion house. As a member of the Versace USA executive team, she led marketing initiatives to support the retail division's new store openings, product introductions, client loyalty programs, and event marketing. Ms. Henderson has worked with the wholesale division to develop marketing programs for all national retailers. She launched the company's global social-media efforts, digital advertising campaign, email marketing, fashion-show live streaming, and blogger network initiative. Most recently, she was responsible for e-commerce for the United States. Prior to joining Versace, she worked at Salvatore Ferragamo in Florence, Italy. During her tenure, she developed and marketed some of the best-performing fragrances in the company's portfolio.

Personal interests include traveling, learning languages, flamenco dancing, running, and reading. Away from work, most of her time is spent with her family.

Christian A. Paul is a career banker with over thirty years of experience. He started his career in 1981 in his native Saint Lucia, and from 1992, he spent the next twenty years moving to different Caribbean countries to take up various roles in the same bank. These postings have helped shape his vast knowledge of financial services.

Mr. Paul has extensive experience in sales management, business development, and intermediary management. He is currently employed with CIBC First Caribbean as the head of International Banking for Barbados operations.

Alfredo Giovine found his home in Barbados after studying and traveling the world for ten years. Italian born, he happily runs his very successful Barbados restaurant in one of the best places in the world—by the sea with a view.

Guy Stanley Philoche is an artist who was born in Haiti and was brought to the United States by his parents at the age of three. After attending Yale University and receiving a master of fine arts degree, he began painting on a full-time basis. His work is widely sought after and appears in a number of corporate, private, and museum collections. He currently resides and works in New York City.

ABOUT THE AUTHOR

Charles A. Archer is passionate about assisting, inspiring, and uplifting everyone he can—especially the disadvantaged. He currently fulfills this mission as CEO of the Evelyn Douglin Center for Serving People in Need, Inc. (EDCSPIN). He and his staff of more than five hundred are dedicated to meeting the needs of more than one thousand developmentally delayed individuals and their families. In his first year as CEO, Charles spoke to his staff about the importance of teamwork, emphasizing that "Everyone Paddles—at the Same Time, in the Same Direction, Toward the Same Goal."© Today, this concept continues to create a cooperative, results-oriented culture at EDCSPIN and has expanded into the "Everybody Paddles" movement.

Charles's education prepared him well for his executive position. In 1996, he earned his bachelor of science degree in business administration and accounting at Lincoln University in Pennsylvania. He then earned a juris doctor degree from Brooklyn Law School in 2001 and became an assistant district attorney in Kings County.

Later, Charles obtained his master of public administration degree from Baruch College, and in 2006, he joined the faculty there, serving as an adjunct professor in the School of Public Affairs. He also became a certified compliance and ethics professional and a certified healthcare compliance professional.

Relishing the opportunity to make the case for services to help those in need, Charles assumed a lobbying role as the associate executive director for the Inter Agency Council of Mental Retardation and Developmental Disability Agencies. Also affiliated with numerous professional associations, he has been called upon to lecture and conduct research on a variety of topics important to organizations that provide policy, leadership, and development support as well as community, day-care, and residential services for the disadvantaged. In 2011, he became a Cuba research delegate with the American Association on Intellectual and Developmental Disabilities, for which he also lectures.

Also in 2011, Charles participated in the Harvard Kennedy School Driving Government Performance Consortium. In early 2012, he received *The Network Journal* 40 Under-Forty Achievement Award for professionals making a significant impact and contribution to the community, and a Leadership Citation from Brooklyn Borough President Marty Markowitz. He was chosen to participate and present at the Division of International Special Education and Services conference in Ireland. The highlight of 2012 was the release of the first edition of *Everybody Paddles: A Guide to Partnership, Association, Collaboration and Togetherness.* A lifelong learner, in the spring of 2014 he was Six Sigma certified through Emory University.

As a self-published author, Charles held launch events and panel discussions in New York City; Washington, D.C.; and Barbados, West Indies. With tremendous support and positive reaction to the "Everybody Paddles" concept, coupled with selling over 1,900 books nationally and internationally, throughout 2013 Charles was able to influence people and discussions around the need to build consensus in diverse areas of endeavor. As a result, Charles received a proclamation for his leadership as the CEO of EDCSPIN from New York City mayor Michael R. Bloomberg.

Along with interests such as running marathons and skydiving, Charles enjoys freelance writing on a wide range of topics, and he has been published in *Mental Health News, City Limits, USA Today,* and on UrbanTimes.com. In addition, he finds time for community service as a member of One Hundred Black Men of New York City, Inc., and a volunteer with

PENCIL, Inc., which inspires innovation and improves student achievement by partnering business leaders with public schools.

Charles serves on the board of directors of Advance of Greater New York; the Brooklyn Chamber of Commerce; Charlottesville Surgical Center; InterAgency Council of Mental Retardation and Developmental Disabilities Agencies; Lutheran Family Health Centers; and Seafarers & International House.

Charles firmly believes that "Everybody is required for everything!" and he is more than willing to do his part.

ENDNOTES

Introduction

1 "Rabbi Hillel Quotes," BrainyQuotes, BookRags Media Network (http://www. brainyquote.com/quotes/authors/r/rabbi_hillel.html), accessed September 25, 2013.

2 "History of the Concept of the Individual and Individuality in Western Society," World Academy of Art and Science (http://www.worldacademy.org/forum/history-concept-individual-and-individuality-western-society), accessed February 14, 2010.

3 "Donald J. Trump," TweetWood, Manusis Technology (http://tweetwood.com/ realDonaldTrump/tweet/286912989322424320), accessed September 25, 2013.

Principle One

1 "Yesterday, When I Was Young," performed by Roy Clark, written by Charles Aznavour; Lyricsmode; Viacom (http://www.lyricsmode.com/lyrics/r/roy_clark/ yesterday_when_i_was_young.html), accessed September 25, 2013.

2 B. R. Ambedkar, BrainyQuote, BookRags Media Network (http://www.brainyquote. com/quotes/authors/b/b_r_ambedkar.html), accessed September 25, 2013.

3 Ray Williams, "Is Gen Y Becoming the New 'Lost Generation'?" *Psychology Today*, April 8, 2013 (http://www.psychologytoday.com/blog/wired-success/201304/ is-gen-y-becoming-the-new-lost-generation), accessed April 3, 2014.

4   Brian Moore, "The Worst Generation?" *New York Post*, May 10, 2010 (http://
     nypost.com/2010/05/10/the-worst-generation/), accessed April 3, 2014.

5   Tom Rath and James K. Harter, *Wellbeing: The Five Essential Elements* (New York:
     Gallup Press, 2010).

6   "Gallup: 'Managers from Hell' Cost US Between $450 Billion to $550 Billion
     Annually," *Daily Caller*, June 25, 2013 (http://dailycaller.com/2013/06/25/gallup-
     managers-from-hell-cost-us-between-450-billion-to-550-billion-annually/),
     accessed April 3, 2014.

7   Cheryl Snapp Conner, "Mentally Strong People: The 13 Things They Avoid," *Forbes*,
     November 18, 2013 (http://www.forbes.com/sites/cherylsnappconner/2013/11/18/
     mentally-strong-people-the-13-things-they-avoid/), accessed April 3, 2014.

8   Helen Keller, The Quotations Page (http://www.quotationspage.com/quote/3141.
     html), accessed September 25, 2013.

9   *"You've Got to Be Carefully Taught," lyrics by Oscar Hammerstein II, music by Richard
     Rodgers; copyright ©1949, Oscar Hammerstein II and Richard Rodgers, renewed;
     Williamson Music, owner of publication and allied rights.*

10   Bruce Piasecki, *Doing More with Teams: The New Way to Winning* (Hoboken, NJ:
     Wiley, 2013).

Principle Two

1   Martin Luther King Jr., BrainyQuote, BookRags Media Network (http://www.
     brainyquote.com/quotes/quotes/m/martinluth105087.html), accessed April 3,
     2014.

2   "Company Fortune 500," Missionstatements.com (http://www.missionstatements.
     com/fortune_500_mission_statements.html), accessed September 25, 2013.

3   James C. Collins and Jerry I. Porras, "Building Your Company's Vision," *Harvard
     Business Review* (http://hbr.org/1996/09/building-your-companys-vision),
     accessed September 25, 2013.

Principle Three

1   Gallup survey cited in Timothy Egan, "Checking Out," *New York Times*, June
     20, 2013 (http://opinionator.blogs.nytimes.com/2013/06/20/checking-out/?_
     php=true&_type=blogs&_r=0), accessed April 4, 2014.

2   Smith cited in Patrick M. Kelley, "How to Identify and Deal with Whining
     Cry Baby (WCB)," LA Sheriff's Organization (http://la-sheriff.org/divisions/
     leadership-training-div/bureaus/dli/assets/dluarticles-kelly.pdf), accessed
     September 25, 2013.

3   Martin Luther King Jr., "Rediscovering Lost Values," The Martin Luther
     King Jr. Papers Project, Stanford University (http://mlk-kpp01.stanford.edu/
     primarydocuments/Vol2/540228RediscoveringLostValues.pdf), accessed
     September 25, 2013.

Principle Four

1   "Pick Yourself Up," written by Jerome Kern and Dorothy Fields, performed by
     Frank Sinatra; copyright © T. B. Harms, Shapiro Bernstein & Co, Inc., Aldi
     Music.

2   Alex "Sandy" Pendleton, "The Hard Science of Teamwork," March 20, 2012
     (http://blogs.hbr.org/2012/03/the-new-science-of-building-gr/), accessed April 11,
     2014.

3   Janine Driver, "The Power of Subliminal Communication," September 23, 2011
     (http://www.doctoroz.com/blog/janine-driver/power-subliminal-communication),
     accessed April 3, 2014.

4   Julius Fast, *Body Language* (New York: Simon & Schuster, 1970).

5   Cited in Jay Yarow, "Larry Ellison Made Steve Jobs Fall Out of His Seat Laughing
     When He Told Him This Story," *Business Insider* (http://www.businessinsider.
     com/gil-amelio-steve-jobs-2011-10), accessed September 25, 2013.

Principle Five

1   Fierce, Inc., survey cited in Phaedra Brotherton, "More Employee Input and
     Accountability Yield More Effective Practices," American Society for Training
     and Development (http://www.astd.org/Publications/Magazines/TD/TD-
     Archive/2012/05/Intelligence-MoreEmployee-Input-and-Accountability-Yield-
     More-Effective-Practices), accessed September 25, 2013.

2   Greenberg cited in Tim Donnelly, "How to Get Feedback from Employees," in
     Inc. (http://www.inc.com/guides/2010/08/how-to-getfeedback-from-employees.
     html), accessed September 25, 2013.

3   Carnegie cited in "Andrew Carnegie Quotes," GoodReads, Inc. (http://www.
    goodreads.com/quotes/251192teamwork-is-the-ability-to-work-together-towards-a-
    common), accessed September 25, 2013.

Conclusion

1   Anthony Robbins, cited in tonyrobbins.com (http://www.tonyrobbins.com/
    resources/ pdfs/2012-Platinum-Partners-Brochure.pdf), accessed September 25,
    2013.